In *Fractured Faith*, Lina shows us that d  and disappointments can ultimately lead faith. Lina gives expression to much of th fear naming. Her transparency, authenticit ......ght lead us to a place of ultimate hope and trust in Jesus, and His never-failing love for us.
**CHRISTINE CAINE,** founder, A21 & Propel Women

In *Fractured Faith*, Lina AbuJamra—ER doc by training and temperament—narrates her painful winnowing through a pastor's betrayal, a church's failure, and a lineup of wolves ready to devour her and whatever other sheep remained. Lina's journey is messy. Some of the things Lina says in this book make me cringe. Survival comes in fits. It grabs at the dark and grabs at the throat. And in the midst of this, we see grace: "the Lord knows how to rescue the godly from trials, and to keep the unrighteous under punishment until the day of judgment" (2 Peter 2:9). *Fractured Faith* points to the glory of God in our weakness and to the Lord's power to keep His true sheep in the grace that we need to finish the race well. Even when our pastors do not measure up. Even when our churches do not measure up. Even when friends prove themselves to be wolves. Even when we do not measure up. Christ always measures up. And that's the point.
**ROSARIA CHAMPAGNE BUTTERFIELD,** author, speaker, homeschool mother

*Fractured Faith* is a special book because it details the pain and promise of what it means to be human. Through unpacking her own story, Lina wrestles with many of the deepest questions in one hand while also doing what she does best: holding God's promises in the other and helping to acknowledge and reframe the pain in a profoundly new light.
**STEVE CARTER,** pastor, author of *The Thing Beneath the Thing*

We've all heard stories of people who have left the church or their faith due to painful circumstances within the body of believers, with people they know and even their experiences with God. If you've ever found yourself in this place and felt like you were too hurt to think about beginning again, I truly hope you will pause to read *Fractured Faith* during this part of your story. In this stunning book, Lina wisely gives voice to the ache many feel. Don't miss this one.
**LYSA TERKEURST,** #1 *New York Times* bestselling author and president of Proverbs 31 Ministries

Stunningly honest. Brilliantly written. Biblically insightful. The questions Lina asks, as she takes us on her journey of deconstructing and then reconstructing her faith, are our questions as well if we dare to be that vulnerable. If you have ever grappled with suffering, doubt, and disappointment in the Christian life, tempted to abandon Christianity completely, read this book. *Fractured Faith* will inspire you to trust Christ in the middle of your story and will reignite your faith. Who should read this book? Everyone I know!

**VANEETHA RENDALL RISNER,** author of *Walking through Fire: A Memoir of Loss and Redemption*

You're not crazy. When your faith is fractured, it's a pain like no other. Through the honest and reflective words of this book, Lina helps you see your brokenness for what it is. But you won't stay where you are. God uses Lina to breathe hope into hurt and revive souls. *Fractured Faith* isn't going to fix you, it's going to start a new fire within you. Hold on!

**KARL CLAUSON,** pastor at 180 Chicago Church; host at *Karl & Crew Mornings*

Lina AbuJamra has written bravely and hopefully in this book. As she's rehearsed betrayals, disappointments, doubts, even her own sin, she's asked a painfully familiar question: Where is God when the lights go out? Retracing a large swath of the biblical story, Lina reminds her readers that God uses every wound, every wilderness, for good.

**JEN POLLOCK MICHEL,** author of *A Habit Called Faith* and *Surprised by Paradox*

I love Lina's passion, Lina's openness, and Lina's constant pursuit of Jesus through His Word. That's what comes through in this deeply encouraging book.

**NANCY GUTHRIE,** author and Bible teacher

One of my biggest burdens I am currently experiencing as a pastor is watching the ever-growing phenomenon of "deconstruction" when it comes to one's faith. I am so grateful that Lina AbuJamra is taking this matter head-on by writing *Fractured Faith*. As the subtitle of the book states, I hope God uses this labor of love to help others find their way back to God in an age of deconstruction. This book was also very beneficial for me as a pastor in understanding how to minister in this new reality. We need this book and I am thankful we now have it, due to Lina's careful, caring, and convicting words. I highly recommend you read *Fractured Faith*.

**DEAN INSERRA,** Founding and Lead Pastor of City Church Tallahassee

As both a writer and reader, I encounter a lot of books, but rarely do they touch me the way Lina AbuJamra's *Fractured Faith* has. Honest yet tender. Simple yet profound. Lina's words are a faithful guide to those who've lost their way or whose faith feels like it's crumbling. Here is hope.

**HANNAH ANDERSON,** author of *Humble Roots* and *Turning of Days*

Written with a beautiful balance of grace and truth, this book was a balm for my wounded heart. Because Lina has walked the path of deep disappointment and doubt, she is a capable guide for those whose faith has been fractured. With a physician's expertise, she invites broken people to the only One who can free us from pain. For anyone wrestling with God or already walking away from the Christian faith, let this book be a lighthouse to help illuminate the way home to the heart of a faithful God whose love is deeper than we can ever imagine.

**DORENA WILLIAMSON,** bridge builder and bestselling author of *ColorFull*

Lina AbuJamra intimately harnesses the pain, fear, and anger that many Christians have felt after the faith bubble has burst. As a leader, she models a brazen authenticity that challenges others to own their part in those emotions. As a believer, she makes a compelling case for faith, more true and more pure than previously experienced in the church. She plainly invites us to see God in the midst of our pain and let go of the pain caused by His people, and perhaps in doing all this, she illuminates a path for countless humans to find their way back to the God who heals.

**CB BARTHLOW,** pastor, son, brother, husband, and father, Denver, CO

In *Fractured Faith*, Lina verbalizes all the feelings and thoughts about my faith, Jesus, and the church that I couldn't seem to personally verbalize over the years. The words of this book helped to unravel the hurt of the past, strengthen my foundation and reignite my passion for Jesus.

**LESLIE,** 33, physical therapist, hurt by the church

*Fractured Faith* is like a lifeline thrown out to a soul drowning in doubt, despair, difficulty, disillusionment, and disappointment, providing a rescue, not with more theological clichés, but with truth shared openly from a heart touched, and still tender, to God's saving grace. Writing with the perfect balance of personal story, memorable illustrations, and scriptural text, the Lord Himself will invite you to come broken and rest in His presence, allowing His truth to settle over you.

JOY, 58, homemaker, restored and redeemed

God uses our brokenness and suffering so we can recover and tell our story with the new understanding that we could only be made whole through the grace and glory of Jesus. Lina's story of brokenness and separation from the church is her testimony of God's grace. If your life is a mess and you feel alone and you want to walk away from God or away from your Christian connections, read this book first. God wants to use your struggle to build a stronger personal relationship with you.

KRISTEN, 55, CFO, Bible Study Fellowship group leader, Prison Ministry volunteer

My soul found a safe place in these beige margins. If this Carpenter she speaks of is real, I want to find Him, too.

ABBIE, unsteady saint, tired homeschool mom

You should buy *Fractured Faith* because it's a truly honest conversation about God, the church, the people in it, and finding our way back to His light when we need it the most.

DALE, 58, Christian CEO, always seeking answers

# FRACTURED FAITH

Finding Your Way Back to God
in an Age of Deconstruction

## LINA ABUJAMRA

**MOODY PUBLISHERS**
CHICAGO

© 2021 by
LINA ABUJAMRA

Unless otherwise indicated, Scripture quotations are from the ESV® Bible (The Holy Bible, English Standard Version®), copyright © 2001 by Crossway, a publishing ministry of Good News Publishers. Used by permission. All rights reserved.

Scripture quotations marked KJV are taken from the King James Version.

All emphasis in Scripture has been added.

Names and details of some stories have been changed to protect the privacy of individuals.

Edited by Amanda Cleary Eastep
Interior Design: Ragont Design
Cover Design: Erik M. Peterson
Cover image of cathedral by Augustine Wong on Unsplash
Author photo credit: Jake Preedin

Library of Congress Cataloging-in-Publication Data

Names: AbuJamra, Lina, author.
Title: Fractured faith : finding your way back to God in an age of
    deconstruction / Lina AbuJamra.
Description: Chicago : Moody Publishers, [2021] | Includes bibliographical
    references. | Summary: "After your faith has fractured, let what takes
    its place be the real thing. Somewhere along the way, the Christianity
    you knew began to crumble. Disillusionment set in. Churches hurt you.
    Their people failed you. Christian institutions were exposed as fake.
    And in it all, God was silent. Is He gone? Or is God really there,
    waiting for you to find Him instead of the counterfeits? If you›re
    walking this spiritual path, Lina AbuJamra understands you. After her
    own faith was nearly lost, Lina had to rebuild something more solid to
    take its place. She›ll help you grapple with questions like: Where is
    God in my pain? Is this how Christians are supposed to act? Why did my
    story end up this way? Let Fractured Faith help you find your way back
    to God. You just might discover that the real God has been waiting for
    you all along"-- Provided by publisher.
Identifiers: LCCN 2021016343 (print) | LCCN 2021016344 (ebook) | ISBN
    9780802422699 | ISBN 9780802499431 (ebook)
Subjects: LCSH: Christian life. | Spirituality--Christianity. |
    Postmodernism--Religious aspects--Christianity. | BISAC: RELIGION /
    Christian Living / General | RELIGION / Christian Living / Social Issues
Classification: LCC BV4501.3 .A248 2021  (print) | LCC BV4501.3 (ebook) |
    DDC 248.4--dc23
LC record available at https://lccn.loc.gov/2021016343
LC ebook record available at https://lccn.loc.gov/2021016344

Originally delivered by fleets of horse-drawn wagons, the affordable paperbacks from D. L. Moody's publishing house resourced the church and served everyday people. Now, after more than 125 years of publishing and ministry, Moody Publishers' mission remains the same—even if our delivery systems have changed a bit. For more information on other books (and resources) created from a biblical perspective, go to www.moodypublishers.com or write to:

Moody Publishers
820 N. LaSalle Boulevard
Chicago, IL 60610

13 5 7 9 10 8 6 4 2

*Printed in the United States of America*

*To Irina*

*who has held my arms up every step of the way.*

*I thank my God upon every remembrance of you.*

# CONTENTS

# PREFACE

I'm actually pretty funny in real life. You will not believe it by reading this book. I've always wanted to write a book that's simple and funny and easy for most people to read. Alas, this book is none of those things. Rather, it is the story of the near collapse of my faith.

At a highlight in my Christian ministry, I hit a wall. You can call it a dark night of the soul or tell me it's a phase that most Christians go through; or you can just read the heart-wrenching truth about what happened to me and let it be a catalyst to help you avoid my mistakes and find hope where you need it.

But one thing you will conclude: This story is anything but funny. This story is anything but easy.

As a pediatric ER doctor I can find humor in almost anything, but most of it is too dark to share out loud and typically only appreciated by others in the emergency room, so I'll spare you the Quentin Tarantino version of my story. Beneath our muffled chuckles, most of us recognize that humor is just another way to hide the pain.

Hiding is never helpful. This book is about coming clean with the truth. It's about the light. It's about the fight for what's good. It's about all the things that matter in this life—things too sacred to rush through, too holy to oversimplify, too precious to laugh hysterically about.

There is a wide range of painful experiences recorded in these pages. I'm not sure where you land on the spectrum of pain, but one thing I believe—God is able to use my serious and sometimes heavy words to touch your heart. I hope He does. I hope you find healing in this book. I hope your faith is reconstructed by His grace. Mine was.

My original working title for this book was *Reconstructing Faith*, but I ran into a problem: my mom couldn't understand why her daughter, a doctor, was writing a book about construction. I tried to explain the concept to her, but if you have a mother, you know how well that went. I ended up changing the title to *Fractured Faith*. A fracture is a break and is incredibly painful. It's the kind of pain that will knock the wind out of you. That's what the deconstruction of your faith will do to you. It knocks the wind out of your faith.

One of the things I've discovered in the last few years is that the deconstructing of one's faith is common among Christians and not just something that happened to me. Christians all over the world are asking difficult questions about their faith. Maybe that's you. You have questions that defy platitudes. Questions that challenge what is taught as dogma in the church. Questions born out of pain that refuse to go away without an answer. They gnaw at your soul and, if they remain unanswered, these questions will lead you down the path to doubt. Then, like a wound that's covered with a bandage without proper care, it starts to fester. Eventually, a dismantling of your beliefs begins to take place. And when everything we believe about God begins to crumble, the temptation is to walk away. The temptation is to stop believing.

Or the very opposite takes place.

Sometimes, when you finally let go of all the clutter you believe about God, you make room for Him in your life again. When you stop long enough for God to reveal Himself to you as He really is and not as you've made Him up to be, a slow reconstruction begins. To help explain this clearly, I created a Deconstruction Diagram (see Appendix) that illustrates the way this often happens in our faith journeys.

It happened to me.

A friend asked me if I could think of anything good that came out of my season of deconstruction. My initial reaction was an adamant No! I wanted to forget every bit of that season in the dark. I thought of all the times I stood up to teach the Bible to others while I was privately wrestling with God, shaking with the shame of being found out. I relived every moment of unshed tears while I fought with God tooth and nail for answers. I mourned so many wasted days in the valley. But then it occurred to me that it was the very deconstruction of my faith that opened my eyes to God. It was the deconstruction of my faith that gave me a taste of His unconditional love and never-ending grace. It was the deconstruction of my faith that rebuilt me inside and out.

Don't get me wrong—I'm still a mess. I still lose my cool when I'm forced to wait too long for a meal. I still see my therapist. And I still struggle with difficult questions. The biggest change in me is that I'm no longer afraid to ask them. I no longer need to hide.

So even though I've promised you that this book will feel heavy at times, here's what else I promise you: if you're struggling with questions about God when you're supposed to already have the answers, and if it feels like you're going through a crisis of faith even after years of following Jesus, I believe you're going to find answers here. But more importantly, I actually believe you might encounter God in these pages, or at least be reminded of His deep, deep love for you.

And someday when you finally come hear me speak in person, I promise that I will not only sign your book, but I'll also make you laugh. But for now, let me tell you about the hardest period of my life.

# MY STORY

The morning I walked away from my church started like any other Sunday morning. I woke up and checked my phone. I scrolled through my favorite apps and made sure all was well in my world. I then got up, made myself a cup of coffee, and sat down at my desk. That's when I remembered that today was the day I had decided to leave my church.

For the average reader this might not sound like a massive declaration, but for any Christian who has walked away from their church, you know exactly the weight I was feeling. Add to that that I was a total insider. I had joined a famous mega-church in Chicago almost a decade earlier and had spent three years working as the leader of the women's ministry. I taught regularly to large groups of women who knew that I had a close relationship with my pastor and his wife. I even had written two books that were coming out that summer. I felt special in those days, chosen and anointed. It was like everything had a purpose in my life. As an insider, I felt like I was at the center of a swelling movement, seated near the warmth of a fire on a cold fall day. It was *something*.

Ten years earlier, I had given my life to serve God in what I thought would be a Bible teaching ministry. I had started a blog that was growing and was gaining more traction with speaking invitations. My relationship with that church seemed like God's added favor on my already blessed life. In those days, *I measured God's goodness to me by the amount of blessings I was experiencing in my life.* I suppose I was living in a mirage I mistakenly called "Christianity."

I didn't decide to leave my church on a whim. For months leading up to that fateful day, my Christian world was slowly disintegrating before my eyes. Several prominent elders had left our church without explanation, and they were blamed for being insubordinate after their departures. Rumors and blog posts about the pastor were popping up everywhere with allegations of abuse of power. I myself had been "disciplined" by the church for an incidental matter and forced to publicly apologize to that pastor. I had witnessed him harshly correct godly men from the pulpit. The tipping point, however, came when a video was shown during the service, chastising some elders because they had confronted the pastor privately on some matters. I knew on that day that something was terribly wrong with that church environment. Even though my proximity to the leader circle had clouded my vision, I recognized a toxicity that did not line up with what I knew about God in His Word. That day I drove home knowing I had to leave. To leave would have certain implications on my future that I couldn't fathom. To stay would be a violation of my conscience.

> I measured God's goodness to me by the amount of blessings I was experiencing in my life.

So, I picked up my phone and quickly sent the text to my former pastor and hero: "Today will be the first time in nine years that I won't be at your church. I have decided to leave and pray you will be well."

I hit send before I had time to rethink my decision. A few seconds later I saw the bubble pop up on my phone, indicating that my pastor was responding. I felt like throwing up as I waited for his response. His text left me feeling manipulated. It also strengthened my resolve to do the right thing and leave.

That Sunday, over six years ago, began the slow deconstruction of my faith. Little did I know at that time how deeply the decision to leave my church would affect my faith. If I could have foreseen the pain that would come from that decision, I am not sure I would have left. If I could have predicted how isolated and abandoned I would feel in the years to come, I likely would have ignored my conscience and gone with the flow. Instead, I chose to lean into disruption; my conscience had finally overruled the status quo. Still, ask anyone who has tried it: *it's never easy to embark on a different road even if that road is the right one.*

The first few months after my split I thought I was okay. I started visiting other churches and eventually landed on attending a big church where I could show up week after week and still go unnoticed. I continued to speak and write about God, with only minor disruptions. When people asked questions about my church story, I came up with a good enough answer to quiet them down, always careful with my words, always frightened that saying the wrong thing might impact my life and ministry. I still felt a pressure to sell the books I had published that summer. I was not naïve about the impact my church decision would have on my life and ministry.

> **It's never easy to embark on a different road even if that road is the right one.**

In those early days, I believed God would step in and do something dramatic to make everything right. I believed God would defend me and reveal the truth about that pastor and his leadership team. I believed God would fix my problems and right wrongs. The longer I waited, however, the more skeptical I became. God didn't appear do anything for a long while.

*Didn't God care about His children?*
*Why wasn't He executing justice where it was due?*
*Where was God in my pain?*

I looked for people to discuss my confusion, but the only ones I found were others who were struggling like I was. They were people like me who had more questions than answers. We recognized each other by the expressions on our faces in the lobbies of the churches we were visiting.

If you've ever left a faith community, you're familiar with that look. It's one of weariness, of self-protection and guardedness. We walk into a room but never quite look people in the eyes. We answer questions with brief affirmatives always giving the impression that we're doing great. "The ministry is thriving," I'd say. "God is working all things out for good," I would declare from the pulpits, time after time.

I believed it at first, until I started to doubt it. Then numbness set in. Numbness beats the struggle over doubt any day of the week. One day I was feeling it all. I was upset and angry and hurt and sad and confused and uncertain. I wondered what went wrong in my life and why I was being treated like the bad person in this narrative when I felt like the victim. I started to question myself: Did I make a mountain out of a molehill? Should I have just sucked it up and stayed? I couldn't quite put my finger on what was at the heart of my angst.

Then it became too much to feel so much, so I chose to go numb. I ignored my emotions. I became an expert on self-isolation and building walls. There's a wall you put up when you don't want anyone to ask you anything, but there's another kind of wall you put up when you want to look like you're engaged in the conversation when in fact you're still just hiding. I call it "my small group wall." It's that thing I do when I pretend to listen and engage with other Christians but my heart and soul stay safely tucked away behind an imaginary barrier. If you're a Christian who has ever attended a small group, you might be familiar with it.

My faith began a slow deconstruction into disbelief. I felt ashamed, ashamed that I'd moved past blaming people to blaming God. Shame that what was once so easy to believe had slowly turned into a crisis of faith. Shame that all the teaching in the world, and all the teaching in the world that I'd taught, hadn't saved me from this crisis of faith, this slow erosion of my faith.

If I could turn back time knowing what I now know, would I have left my church that sacred Sunday morning six years ago? Ask me on a tough day when I'm feeling particularly vulnerable and self-protective, and I don't think I would have. I would have chosen the comfort of safety. But I've learned that it takes guts to lean into the truth. It takes grit and the willingness to live honestly to admit the struggle you're feeling. It will take everything in you to learn how to be your true self.

For decades, I thought I had all the answers. I thought I was living honestly, but in reality, I had just shaped my life to be what everyone around me expected it to be. For decades, I thought I was living my true self. Some people live for the glory of self. During that time of my life, I still lived for the approval of other people. It took a crisis of faith for me to admit that what I had called my "true self" was only a fractured self, modeled after human understanding, not after God. It took a crisis of my faith—a deconstruction of my faith—to show me that what I had called my true self was anything but true.

Your story may not be church-related at all. Your pain may be much more personal. Your hurt may have been born out of deep abuse. Your struggle may be the result of repetitive disappointment and unshakable bad "luck." Your wounds may be the result of something you did or something that was done to you. Your skepticism may be due to your dissatisfaction with the standard answers you've heard to life's most difficult questions. That's okay. While it matters to recognize where we've been, it's much more important to know where we're going. And as you come on this journey with me, I will give you no trite answers and we'll avoid boring pit stops. We're marching toward wholeness. We're banking on freedom.

You can choose to stay the course you're on; it might even be easier for you in the short run. Just shut this book and you're done. Same old, same old. But if you're sick of feeling stuck in your painful circumstances, this book will help you see a pathway to your purpose in your pain. If you're exhausted trying to control the outcomes in your life, we're going to talk about how your hurt is holding you back and how to release it.

In the next pages I'm going to explore five things that almost destroyed my faith in God:

Suffering
Expectation
Rejection
Surrender
Justice

I'm going to tell you why, and I'm going to help you redefine those five words. I'm going to help you find answers to your questions about God. I know that's promising a lot, but I believe I can deliver. The reason is that I'm here, typing these words when it's the last thing I would have chosen. Today, I believe again, and I'm going to help you get there too.

Oh, and one more thing: you might think this book is about finding your way back to God, but it's not. It's about understanding that God has already found His way to you.

# Chapter 1

# WHERE IS GOD IN MY PAIN?

I've heard a million sermons about suffering. I bet you have too. You'd think I'd know all about suffering by now. You'd think I'd have figured out how to assimilate my suffering into a clean Christian box of faith. But that's not my story, and since you're reading this book, it's probably not your story either.

As an ER doctor, I've lived with pain my whole professional life—that is, other people's pain. And while it bothers me to see them hurt, let me tell you about the day my eight-year-old nephew was brought to the ER with abdominal pain. I happened to be the attending physician in the ER that day. An hour later my nephew was in the ER, crying in pain, though at sixteen today, he would rather die than admit it. Suddenly my knowledge about pain flew out the window. *This* pain was personal.

Humans suffer. It's a fact of life, like breathing. Most of us are compassionate enough to admit our frustration with human suffering in general. But the biggest questions we have about God are born out of personal pain.

Where is God in *my* pain? Why does He seem so far away when *I* need Him the most? Most sermons I've heard about suffering offer clear scriptural assertions that God is always with us. My heart rejoices when I hear that no good thing will God withhold from those who walk uprightly (Ps. 84:11), or that no weapon formed against me will succeed (Isa. 54:17). Yet the euphoria and reassurance barely last through Sunday brunch until I'm alone with my thoughts again, wondering if I'm the only Christian still asking, "Why?"

*Why does this hurt so much?*
*Why can't I hear God's whisper in the darkness?*

I need more than tweetables and popular hashtags when I'm hurting. In the valley of the shadow of death, I need to *know* that I follow a Savior who is not oblivious to my pain.

> **The key is in remembering who God really is, not who we've made Him to be.**

Ironically, God is not unfamiliar with our cry for His presence when we're overwhelmed with suffering. Since the creation of humankind, God has heard it all. He's heard our complaining and our accusations. He's heard our moans and our groans. He's heard our confusion and our frustrations. He's not unaware of our pain though it may seem like it at first. In fact, the story of the Bible is the story of the suffering of humankind and the goodness of a God who saves them—and almost always *despite* them. The story of the Bible is the story of an imperfect people and their good God—a God who sometimes seemed to be missing in the middle of their pain, but somehow showed up when they least expected Him to and in ways they never anticipated.

In other words, just when we take God out of the equation, He shows up with so much goodness it's hard to ignore. The key is often in learning to know what to look for in our pain. *The key is in remembering who God really is, not who we've made Him to be.*

The Bible is a beautiful display of humanity in all of its pain and glory. The writers do not attempt to hide or minimize the flaws of humankind. If anything, it seems as if they revel in telling all the ugly details. Throughout this book I'm going to tell the biblical accounts of men and women like us—men and women with questions and struggles. Men and women with disappointments and doubts. Men and women who thought the worst about God and faced the truth about themselves. Men and women whose faith almost eroded, who hung on to it by a thread, and who later had their faith miraculously reconstructed. Men and women who are going to help us better understand our own struggles to believe.

### Meet Naomi

At the top of my list of favorite untidy stories in the Bible is the story of a woman named Naomi. Her life got so bad that at one point she told everyone she knew that she was changing her name from Naomi to Mara, which means bitter. But Naomi's story, like so many of our stories, didn't start out bad. It just got bad, and when things looked even worse, God seemed absent.

Naomi was married to a man named Elimelech. They were both followers of the God of Abraham. They had two sons, Mahlon and Chilion. A famine struck their land so the family decided to emigrate to Moab. If you're a Bible scholar, you might have a solid critique of their move, but if you're human like me, you might figure that their move was an act of survival. If you're a Bible scholar, you probably know that the Moabites were not friendly to God, and that Naomi and Elimelech ought to have known better. But most of us understand the need to reach for security when faced with our own seasons of famine.

I grew up in West Beirut in the 1970s and 1980s. Those were years of severe famine, and when famine strikes, people run. Only the lucky ones could escape. The war made it hard to survive in a city that had been considered the Paris of the Middle East. I don't remember Beirut looking anything like Paris. But I do remember the bullet holes in buildings and the weeks spent in the hallway of our home praying that the bombs and the shrapnel wouldn't kill us. We were one of the families that eventually escaped. Given a chance to emigrate to the United States, we took it. So, when I hear that Elimelech and Naomi ran away from the famine, it's hard to criticize their decision. With two young men to raise and their hunger palpable, running seems very palatable. I totally get that.

Still, Naomi and Elimelech's decision seemed to backfire. Before long, Elimelech died and soon afterwards, both of Naomi's sons died too. As if life couldn't get any harder, she was left with two daughters-in-law. Desperate and broken, Naomi decided to go back home. Her daughters-in-law, maybe out of a sense of duty or guilt, started out with her. But it didn't take long for the first one, Orpah, to bail. Who could blame her? The other daughter-in-law, however, stuck around. Her name was Ruth. Unbeknownst to Naomi, Ruth would become the tipping point in Naomi's life. *It's in learning to become aware of God's presence in our pain that the scales are tipped toward freedom.* Yet in the midst of this famine, neither Ruth nor Naomi could have predicted how life would play itself out.

By the time Naomi got back to her hometown of Bethlehem, she was a mess. And she was in pain, so she changed her name to Mara. Her arrival back home was no small affair. We're told that "when they came to Bethlehem, the whole town was stirred because of them" (Ruth 1:19). Were they stirred in pity? Were they stirred in self-righteousness? Were they stirred in shock? We'll never know, but we're given a glimpse as to how Naomi felt in her pain. She was hurting and likely felt vulnerable, exposed, and fragile.

"Do not call me Naomi; call me Mara, for the Almighty has dealt very bitterly with me. I went away full, and the Lord has brought me back empty. Why call me Naomi, when the LORD has testified against me and the Almighty has brought calamity upon me?" (Ruth 1:20–21).

Have you ever felt like God was against you? Like He went missing when you needed Him the most? Have you ever felt alone in your pain? That was Naomi's experience, in a nutshell.

My friend understands that feeling. She grew up in a Christian home, went to a Christian high school, and then graduated from a Christian college. Afterwards, she moved back home and eventually married and started a family. She couldn't have been happier. Then her husband had an affair, and they divorced. Today, she no longer believes in God.

I've asked her why: Why did she stop believing?

"God wasn't there in my pain. When I went through the divorce, I looked for God, but He wasn't there," she said. "So, I stopped believing." In the middle of her deepest pain, my friend felt abandoned by God. She became an unbeliever, and I sympathize with her.

Pain has a way of revealing who you really are and what you really believe. Pain doesn't destroy your faith; it simply exposes it. Instead of seeing pain and suffering as the worst thing that could happen to you, it's life-saving to see suffering as a pathway to God. *Instead of allowing suffering to deconstruct your faith, consider how God wants to use your suffering to reignite your faith in Him.*

I've done a lot of healing in the last six years to be able to write these words: I joined a small group recently. It's an interesting and eclectic group of people who share two main things in common: Jesus and a group thread. I woke up to this text recently from one of the small group members:

"This new solo life is tough—just divorced four years and not used to being single, and seeing your adult child still broken is tough. I am realizing that I'm still grappling with my anger with God. Intellectually I know I don't deserve anything, and anything He gives us is sheer grace but in my heart I still feel hurt and keep scratching my head at the things He allows or disallows."

If you've ever felt the sting of disappointment and pain, it's not hard to wrap your mind around my friend's words: *Doesn't God care enough about me to end my suffering?*

It wasn't just people in the Old Testament who struggled to see God in their pain. Even while Jesus was alive, those who were closest to Him wondered whether He was aware of their suffering. One time, Jesus got on a boat with His disciples after a busy day of ministry. While He slept in the back of the boat, a storm broke out, "and the waves were breaking into the boat, so that the boat was already filling" (Mark 4:37). The disciples were horrified. They were angry, frustrated, and confused. They woke Jesus up none too gently and expressed their surprise at Him: "Teacher, do you not care that we are perishing?" (v. 38).

> *God, don't You care that we're in pain?*
> *Don't You see what we're going through?*
> *Don't You understand that we're sinking?*
> *How can You sleep while we're hurting?*

Who of us hasn't faced the agony of feeling abandoned by the Almighty in our hour of deepest need? Remember Mary and Martha in John 11? They did all the right things. They lived for Jesus. They loved Him and were loved by Him. When they hit troubled waters and their brother Lazarus got sick, they looked to Jesus. They believed He could heal him. They believed He *would* heal him. They figuratively circled the verse in their Bibles and prayed. They begged Jesus for their miracle. They hoped for an answer to their prayers. They wanted healing from their pain. But instead of showing up in their hour of despair, Jesus did the very opposite.

"When he heard that Lazarus was ill, he stayed two days longer

26

in the place where he was" (John 11:6). By the time Jesus did show up, Lazarus had died.

What kind of Savior does that? What kind of Savior holds back when His people—those whom He loves—need Him the most? *What kind of Savior chooses silence over comfort? Absence and delay over the miracle? What kind of Savior allows His children to be swept away in the storms of life, seemingly oblivious to their pain?*

## God, Are You There?

I'm not a theologian; I'm a doctor. If you have a problem, I want to fix it and fix it fast. I typically know exactly what to do, and I can do it in record time. It's why people come to me for help. Even in real life, when I'm not in the ER, I think on my feet. My kind of thinking makes me annoying to the contemplative types and Enneagram 2s. (If you don't know what the Enneagram is, don't worry, you'll survive and it won't lessen the impact of this book for you.) I tend to think in black and white, yeses and noes, and simple answers that, according to one reviewer of my first book, *Thrive*, can sound to some people "theologically trite."

Maybe I am trite, or maybe I just have a yearning to fix everyone's problems. And fast! The fact that I love concrete, clear answers to problems makes the mysteries, complexities, and nuances of the Christian life immensely challenging to me at times. Yet, it is in complicated questions where we find the truth. We need to ask the tough questions, such as:

> *Why does Jesus sleep in the middle of the storm?*
> *Why does Naomi lose all the men in her life?*
> *Why doesn't Jesus show up when Mary and Martha need Him the most?*
> *Where was God in my friend's painful divorce?*

*Why do I still find it challenging to talk about the pain inflicted on me by my old church?*

I've spent the last five years working with Syrian refugees in the Middle East. It's been one of the best things I've done in my life. The work came unexpectedly and unintentionally. I had just left my church and was coming to terms with all the losses in my life. I wasn't sure what I'd do with the rest of my life. I looked for God in my pain, but instead of finding Him in the places I wanted Him to be, all I found was an invitation to do this work with a people that I had grown up hating, but had come to love. (More on *that* later, I promise.)

I got on a plane and went back home to my birth country to run my first medical clinic serving Syrian refugees who had fled from the terror of ISIS. I found a people whose pain made mine pale in comparison. I found a people who hurt so badly, no earthly balm could ever soothe them. I found a people who had lost everything—loved ones, home, security, comfort, respect, jobs, futures, and dreams.

Yet, in the midst of their pain, many of them had also found life and freedom. Many of them had found joy and the realization that life was more than food and clothing. In the midst of their pain, many of them had found Jesus.

I remember the first time I met Daria (not her real name). She was beaming. There's no other way to describe her. She had a smile that shone for miles. I wanted her to be my friend simply because of her radiance. I found out that she was a Syrian refugee who had started working at the church, cooking and cleaning for visitors like me. She had first been introduced to the church because of her physical needs. Her family was hungry and the church was giving out food rations to those in need. So, she showed up wearing her hijab, convinced she would be turned away. Her kids fell in love with the children's programs that were offered and kept coming back for more. Her eldest, an eleven-year-old boy with soulful eyes, heard about Jesus and couldn't resist His love for him. He wouldn't stop talking about Him. He'd encountered the risen Christ and his whole life changed. His family noticed the difference. Daria tried her best to shut him up. Frustrated when he refused to give up, she stormed to the church ready to meet this man named Jesus who had created such havoc in her home.

She walked into the church intent on meeting this Jesus and, sure enough, she did. She walked back home with a new life, a new love, a new heart, and a new perspective. In the midst of her pain, Daria had found the Messiah, or maybe He'd found her. In the midst of her pain, she found freedom, and her joy became palpable to anyone who would meet her. Eventually her husband would believe in Christ as well. Today, Daria knows Jesus; He redeemed her pain and replaced it with the joy of His presence.

Daria is still a refugee. Her home has not been recovered yet, and tragically probably never will be. She has not gotten a great education or graduated from college. She hasn't won the lottery. She lives with the reality of the broken pieces of her life, yet I have never met anyone happier or more satisfied in their life. I have never met anyone more aware of God's presence.

How is it that so many Syrian refugees meet God in their pain and find Him while so many of us in the West sink into despair in our seasons of (metaphorical) famine? Do they simply look for Him a little bit harder? Do they need Him more than they need their prayers answered and their dreams fulfilled? Perhaps they've finally gotten to the place where they have run out of prayer ideas. Having hit rock bottom, anything will do, and a Savior who promises life and freedom and resurrection that can never be taken away becomes so obviously the answer.

Perhaps it is our many desires for material comfort that have sidetracked us from what our soul really needs. Perhaps we can learn something important from refugees like Daria: Suffering is not the worst thing that can happen to a person but, instead, can be an invitation to the heart of our Savior.

*The longer I live, the more I wonder if my inability to see God in my pain is rooted in the fact that I'm not really looking for God. I'm looking for a god to show up in the way that I want him to and to give me what I want him to give me.* I'm like the disciples; I beg Jesus to stop my storm *now*. I'm like Mary and Martha; I want Jesus to heal my sick brother *now*.

Some like to think that because Jesus suffered once, we never will have to. That because Jesus was wounded, we're promised permanent healing; that if He was abandoned by God, we never will be. But what if the very fellowship of His suffering is meant to draw us closer to Him? What if our very pain is meant to help us see Him more clearly?

Why do some people turn to God in their pain while others turn away from Him? C. S. Lewis once wrote that "God whispers to us in our pleasures, speaks in our conscience, but shouts in our pain: it is His megaphone to rouse a deaf world."[1] But I'm left to wonder, if pain is God's megaphone to rouse a deaf world, why do so many of us remain oblivious to God's presence in our pain? Why is it so hard to hear Him when we need Him the most?

We have a Savior who is quite familiar with our suffering. We have a Savior who understands what we're going through in our pain. *The reality is that often we're never as close to our Father as we are in our suffering. We're never as alive to God's purposes as we are when we suffer.* We just have to learn to see it more clearly. We just have to learn to live in awareness of God's presence even in our pain—or *especially* in our pain. (Don't worry. I'm going to tell you how I've learned to do so. Just keep reading.)

## Waking Up to God's Presence

If there's one word I've learned to hate, it's the word COVID-19. By the time this book will be released, most of us will have become quite familiar with the effects of a global pandemic. Most of us think of "suffering" when we hear the word COVID-19, but as an ER doctor turned telehealth provider, I hear "awareness."

COVID-19 has brought awareness like few other things have. Because of this deadly virus, we as humans have become aware of distances—six feet being the magical distance needed between two people for adequate protection. Because of COVID-19, we have become aware of the need to cover our mouths when we cough and wash our hands for twenty seconds multiple times a day. We are aware of others when they cough now. The pain of COVID-19 has created a heightened awareness of our own humanity, interconnection, and need. *Pain's gift is that it increases awareness. Suffering heightens our sense of need and deepens our heart's cry for help. While suffering hurts, a growing sense of God's presence heals.*

The longer I live as a Christian the more I am convinced that God saved, and saves, us despite ourselves, both on the cross as well as now, each and every day. The formulas that used to work for me don't anymore. Answers that have long served the purpose of quieting my questions now fall on jaded ears like water on a duck. They wet the surface of my heart but they don't penetrate deeply.

These days I need more than just three steps to get there. I need the reality of God's presence. I need the truth about God. I need a God who will save me on my worst days—even when I know better. The good news of the gospel is that we have such a God in Jesus. But that good news of the gospel is still ours to be received. God's goodness is meant to be received in the midst of our pain, not proven by the absence of our pain.

> **God's goodness is meant to be received in the midst of our pain, not proven by the absence of our pain.**

One of the ways I have learned to grow in my awareness of God is to practice seeking His presence with a very simple prayer that I whisper to God throughout the day. It's a prayer any kid can memorize, which is about the level I can handle when I'm crushed by suffering. Though I don't believe in secret formulas or chants that empower us to be more for God, I have found this whispered prayer awakens me to God's presence in my life:

*Lord,*
*Open my eyes that I may see You.*
*Open my ears that I may hear You.*
*Open my mouth that I may praise You.*
*Open my heart to receive all that You have for me today.*

Living in the reality of God's presence is not meant to be difficult. It's meant to be freeing. It's meant to ignite hope. It's meant to be real. I hope this prayer helps you too.

### The End of Pain

There's one more thing I learned from the story of Naomi: It's that no matter how bad today is, eventually harvest does come. After bemoaning her fate and expressing her frustration with God, we're told that "Naomi returned, and Ruth the Moabite her daughter-in-law with her . . . and they came to Bethlehem at the beginning of barley harvest" (Ruth 1:22).

There is significance to the mention of harvest after years of famine. At the depth of Naomi's grief, the mention of harvest is God's offer of hope in a season of pain. Harvest was a reminder of God's presence, the evidence of His powerful hand of provision. For Ruth and Naomi, harvest meant the beginning of a new season and the end of the old. That year Ruth became the catalyst for healing. Ruth went out to harvest, and of all the fields she could have chosen, she chose Boaz's. Boaz would become the kinsman-redeemer for Ruth and Naomi. The kinsman-redeemer in those days was a male relative who had the privilege or responsibility to act on behalf of a relative who was in trouble or need. He was meant to be a redeemer or deliverer for the needy. Boaz would do just that on the day he would marry Ruth, but it was ultimately God who had orchestrated that season of harvest that year. And it was Naomi who experienced new life.

God's goodness is first glimpsed at the beginning of harvest even when we still feel bitter or, fittingly, "mara." No matter how hopeless today feels, light is on the way, and it has less to do with what I do and everything to do with who God is. He is good. He is sovereign. If you're in a season of pain, it might feel foreign for you to read those words. It might feel like a cruel joke to hear that light is making its way beneath the crack in your doorway. But it's the truth. You might be praying for fruit right now, but perhaps God's plan for today is the grain that will yield your harvest someday down the road. Daria understands it; even I understand it.

It took a while for me to see my season of harvest come. I was one whose faith almost deconstructed in the pain. I became suspicious of God. I became hardened in my heart. I went through the motions, did the right things, but I resented this God who seemed so far away. Some days I felt angry. Other days I felt grief. I'd numb my pain or distract myself with Netflix and other addictions. I dared God to stop me. I yelled at anyone who would listen. I almost fell off the proverbial cliff. The people in my life tried to placate me with well-meaning answers, but this was a battle I was waging with God.

It wasn't about them; it was between me and this God whom I barely understood anymore.

People talk about the dark night of the soul. The sixteenth-century Spanish mystic and poet St. John of the Cross experienced that dark night and then wrote two books about the concept.[2] It wasn't about suffering, but about being guided to God, even through our difficulties. I don't know if what I lived through was a dark night of my soul or Satan trying to take me out. All I know is that what seemed familiar, reliable, and certain in my twenties and thirties had become foreign and stale to me in my forties. I thought about leaving the faith. I stopped going to church for a while.

Yet something kept me hanging on. I felt tethered to a force bigger than me. For a while I lived in Genesis 32. If you're not familiar with the story, it's the one where Jacob wrestles with God in the middle of the night. He fights with everything he's got for a while, but eventually, he wears out. I'm not sure if he wanted to let go at one point, but somehow, he hung on. Or maybe it was *God's* hold on *him*.

I've read the story of Jacob a thousand times, and I can't quite tell when the turning point in that night was. The only thing I can see is that when Jacob wore out, when he couldn't fight God anymore, he let go. He had no plan B, no way out of his mess. That's when God took over.

I have a feeling it was Jacob's letting go, rather than hanging on, that saved him.

Most of us intuitively understand that there is "a time to plant, and a time to pluck up what is planted; a time to kill, and a time to heal; a time to break down, and a time to build up; a time to weep, and a time to laugh; a time to mourn, and a time to dance" (Eccl. 3:2–4).

Eventually harvest will come and with it a season of dancing and rejoicing.

## Unexpected Joy

When harvest comes it usually comes in unexpected and unusual ways. For Naomi, the harvest came through community, and specifically a daughter-in-law named Ruth who would eventually birth a boy who would become a forebear of Jesus. For others, the harvest comes through a miracle, like Jesus' whisper stilling the storm. Sometimes harvest comes through a resurrection, like it happened for Lazarus. Or it may come quietly, unexpectedly, in the form of an empty tomb on a Sunday morning when everyone has already written that story off.

In the middle of the darkness, God's light still shines. In the midst of our pain, His sovereign goodness overrules our pain. It turns out that God is committed to us, despite us.

For me things got messier before they got better. Breakthrough came through the unexpected form of God's people. Though it was God's people who had hurt me, they became the tool God used to heal my broken heart. A loving pastor who wouldn't give up on me. His wife who understood me. A small church community who saw past my defenses. *Though it was God's people who fueled the deconstruction of my faith, it was also God's people who would become the building blocks for its reconstruction.*

Then there was my therapist. For the first time in my life, I was given the chance to tell the truth, the whole truth, and nothing but the truth. It took my going to a therapist to finally find the safety to tell the truth.

I told the truth about my pain. I told the truth about my anger. I told the truth about my relationship with God. I told the truth about everything.

And then I cried. I cried over my broken heart. I cried over the pain inflicted by my lost community. I cried over my dead dreams and lonely days. I cried over everything I could think of. She listened until I stopped crying. She told me it was okay. She accepted who I was. And she pointed me to the One my heart still longed for.

And I realized an earth-shattering truth: In the middle of my suffering, God was still right there. He had never left me. He had never abandoned me. Just like He'd promised, even when I tried to make my bed in hell, He was right there with me all along (Ps. 139:8). Just because I hadn't noticed God's presence didn't make His presence any less real. It took my hitting rock bottom to notice that when I'd lost my grip on God, He'd kept His grip on me, and He resurrected hope in me.

The first step to reconstructing your faith is to start by telling the truth. You need to find a safe place to tell your story, like to a therapist or trusted pastor or friend. It's essential. And it will not be pretty. You don't need to hide anymore. You don't need to act like everything is okay. You are in this fight because you have questions, and they're not a surprise to God. Your present suffering is God's invitation to you for more of His presence in your life. It will take courage and guts to tell your story. It might even create some significant changes in your future, but it will be worth it. You will find out that you are not alone in your pain, and that when you finally let it all out, God will still be right there, waiting for you. You will realize that God isn't disturbed by your pain. He welcomes it; He welcomes you. He's a Savior who is familiar with our pain. But He's also a Savior who knows that glory is born out of suffering. If you feel like you've lost your grip on God, it's okay to let go. Because when you finally let go, you'll find that He still has His grip on you.

Today, you might be asking, "Where is God in my pain?" but try to believe, even for a moment, that tomorrow your harvest is coming.

**SPEND A FEW MINUTES CONSIDERING THESE QUESTIONS,**
**and bring your thoughts and feelings to God in prayer:**

*Do you relate to the story of Naomi? Which part feels most familiar to you?*

*Are you aware that God is with you in your pain?*

*Can you make room for God's whispers in your grief?*

*Chapter 2*

# WHY DID MY STORY END UP THIS WAY?

When I was in medical school, one of my classmates came to the mind-boggling realization that after four years of college and two years in medical school, he didn't really like medicine after all. What he thought would be a life he would love turned out to be nothing but trouble. By that time, he was so far in debt that the idea of leaving school wasn't even an option. Though he still had two more years to go, he dared not tell anyone of his struggle. In fact, most of us didn't find out until almost graduation that this guy stopped wanting to be a doctor years before, but he was stuck.

My friend kept going through the motions. He showed up to class day after exhausting day. He studied like the rest of us did and took care of his patients week after week. He passed the exams and dissected his cadaver. Though he looked like the rest of us, he had a secret: he didn't want to be a doctor anymore. A life in medicine wasn't what he expected it to be.

I've come to find out that most of us go through life exactly like my classmate did. We wake up one day and realize that all we once held dear no longer matters to us anymore. We thought our story would turn out one way, but instead we're stuck in a life that doesn't seem like the one we deserve. The problem is that we're too afraid to admit it. We're frightened of what it might mean to admit it. So we show up. We go through the motions. We live, but we're not really alive. We inhale and exhale, but we're not really breathing.

We think nobody notices, but the signs are everywhere. They're in our smiles that don't quite reach our eyes. They're in the heaviness we carry with us wherever we go. They're in the hunch in our shoulders and the drag of our legs. We've led ourselves to believe that there is a virtue in just showing up, that somehow God will eventually reward our tenacity. And maybe He will. Maybe there is something to be said about just not quitting.

But, year after year, the cost on our soul grows. Without noticing, we become anemic and inauthentic. Some might even accuse us of being hypocrites. We say we're one thing, and we live one narrative, but inside, we're rotting. Have you ever left a container of yogurt in your fridge for too long? I know, I know. No one knows exactly how long is too long for a container of yogurt, but most of us would agree that a couple of years may be too long. Anyway, that yogurt looks okay on the outside. It sits happily on the shelf until you open it. Then if you're still alive from the smell that explodes, you're certain to die if you taste it.

**When our Christianity hasn't lived up to our expectations, it's important to stop and figure out why.**

I am convinced that more people in the church are struggling with their faith than are letting on. These are people who, like me, still go to church and read their Bibles daily but are slowly shriveling inside. We look okay on the outside, but inside we're dying. We're afraid to admit that the Christian life we're living isn't what we expected it to be. *When our Christianity hasn't lived up to our expectations, it's important to stop and figure out why.*

Are we expecting the wrong things? Is our disappointment in

the Christian life legitimate? Or could there be more beneath the surface? Could God be using our unmet expectations to propel us into a specific purpose? What if our expectations were merely a tool meant to draw us closer to God instead of further away from Him?

Instead, many who wrestle with their faith simply quit. They leave the church looking for something else, somewhere else. They try to convince themselves that they still love Jesus, but inside a shift has begun. Their faith is eroding. Young men and women who grow up hearing about God the promise maker and God the promise keeper find themselves with a bag of empty promises, their lives a shell of what they expected God to do for them. If God indeed has failed to deliver what He has promised, no wonder over fifty percent of millennials have left the church.[1] If God has indeed not lived up to our expectations, no wonder more people claim to be religiously unaffiliated than ever before.[2]

Maybe you're struggling with your faith right now. Maybe nobody knows it except you so far—and, well, God. You've gotten really good at playing the game. You show up to church, you serve, you host a small group, you even sing in the choir. You bring your Bible to church every week. But you know it. You can't escape it. It's like my friend not wanting to be a doctor anymore; you feel stuck.

What if instead of coming to God with your expectations, you learned to come to Him with your longings? What if you brought your doubts, your dashed hopes, and your desires to God, trusting that He loves you and wants your story to have a hope-filled ending?

## What *Do* You Truly Expect?

My mother once told me that she believed God told her that I would have a baby someday.

To be honest, I never thought much about it in my early years. I assumed that one day I would grow up and get married and have kids.

It wasn't even something I spent time worrying about.

But my mom had different thoughts about it. She had seen me suffer. When I was eight years old, I developed severe lower abdominal pain. I woke my parents up in the middle of the night with my groans. My father, a plastic surgeon, saw the signs of a surgical problem and we headed to the emergency room. Everyone thought it was the appendix. This was back in 1980, before CT scans and ultrasounds. The surgeon ended up starting the incision in the right lower quadrant of my abdomen only to see a normal appendix. He kept on cutting until he found the problem, way over on my left ovary.

I woke up and found out I'd lost both my appendix and my left ovary in the process. The incident didn't impact me so much as an eight-year-old, but my mom was shaken. I got my period when I was thirteen when I was away at a summer camp and was mortified to have to tell my mom about it over the phone. The entire ordeal was traumatizing for me. Today, all I remember about it was the joy in her voice when she heard the news that I had actually "become a woman."

It was almost ten years after my first broken engagement that I got engaged again. Around that time my mother accidentally slipped and told me about a word she had received from the Lord. She shared how she felt that God had promised her that despite the pain of my surgery, He would grant me a child someday. That promise had filled her with joy and expectation. A few weeks later, instead of moving forward with the wedding and granting my mom a future grandchild, my engagement ended.

I still have never gotten married and have never had a child. Some days I feel guilty about it. Should I have gone through with the wedding in the hopes of fulfilling my mom's dream for me? While my mother has not brought up this conversation again in my life, I've often wondered about God in all this. Why would God give my mom a promise only to let her down in time? Why would God fail to meet my mom's expectation when her desire seemed to be so good? And through it all, what was the longing in my mother's heart that led to that expectation in her relationship with God? Was she hearing her own desire or a word from God?

We all have longings, desires, and wants. We have dreams and expectations. We expect God to meet our desires; we expect Him to fulfill our deepest longings. When our lives and even our faith in Christ haven't lived up to our expectations, it's important to stop and figure out why. To do so, we must begin by making the connection between longing, desire, and expectation.

Purely speaking, "to expect" is to look forward to with anticipation. When a pregnant woman is expecting, she is looking forward with anticipation to having a child. Her expectation for a safe delivery grows out of her longing for a healthy child. First comes our desires, which drive our longings. Another way to say it is that our longings are our delayed desires. And then come our expectations. Our expectations are our anticipated outcomes. Our expectations are less attached to our desires and more connected to our anticipated narratives. I might desire success but expect to lose. Expectations are too often influenced by our fears. Expectations are shaped by our past with all of its wounds and regrets. We tend to taper our expectations to protect ourselves from future pain even though we long for our desires so deeply we can almost taste them.

The problem with expectations is that they can make or break our faith. Prayer in its simplest form is coming to God with our expectations, being honest with God, holding our expectations loosely, inviting God to give us the desire of our hearts and what He most desires for us. As long as our expectations are based on God's promises, our happiness is sure to be complete. Those kinds of expectations will always bring delight because they rest in God's character and in His goodness. Our problems start when—with tight fists—we bring God expectations that hinge on our own wants and desires, often centered around our own comfort and perceived happiness, regardless of what He might want for us.

It is in better understanding our desires that we can form our expectations. What is it that we really want? What is it that we long for? Or maybe a better question we must ask is: How well can we trust our longings and our desires? What might God be showing us He wants for us?

### Let's Start at the Very Beginning

The story of God is a story of desire. God created a perfect world in Genesis and put two perfect people in it. Their names were Adam and Eve. They had everything they could ever want, except for one thing. In that garden was a tree, the tree of knowledge of good and evil, and it had fruit on it. God gave Adam and Eve free rein over the entire garden of Eden except for that one tree. God told Adam and Eve not to eat of the tree of knowledge of good and evil because it would harm them. Two chapters into the story of God, Eve became consumed with her desire for the one thing she couldn't have. She longed for the forbidden fruit. Her expectation was that God should allow her to have that fruit simply because she wanted it. She ignored God's warning and chose her desire over everything else in the world. She chose her hunger for that fruit over God.

That day sin entered the world. That day became known as the fall of humankind. I'm sure you're familiar with the story but maybe you haven't connected its impact on your life. Because of that day, you and I will always wrestle with our desires. We long, and sometimes our longings are good, but often, they're not. The only way to tell the difference is by weighing our desires by what God has promised will give us lasting happiness. We must learn to discern the difference. Failure to do so has some serious implications as Adam and Eve found out. Their choices led them to hide in shame and separate themselves from the One who loved them and had created them for wholeness.

I have a lot of desires, or wants, in my life—some positive and some negative. I sometimes want to hang up on patients who treat me disrespectfully. I sometimes want to eat an entire pint of ice cream. I sometimes want to hurt people who hurt me. But I have desires that better align with my faith too. I desire to feed more Syrian refugees. I desire to be gentler and kinder to strangers. I desire to live a healthy life. I desire to have deep and meaningful relationships with others. You can make your own list of positive and negative desires; it's a good exercise. It can be entered into as a spiritual practice, one that can draw us nearer to God.

Our hearts are divided between good desires and evil desires. It was James, the brother of Jesus, who wrote in his short letter to the church in the New Testament what the root of every evil desire is: "Each person is tempted when he is lured and enticed by his own desire. Then desire when it has conceived gives birth to sin, and sin when it is fully grown brings forth death" (James 1:14–15).

Because of Adam and Eve, we have inherited this desire for sin which leads to death. But because of Jesus we've been given the desire for life and goodness. Again, the key is to recognize the difference between positive and negative desires.

## My Struggle with Desire

Let me try to illustrate the tension between desire and expectation by sharing my own struggle with desire.

As I write these words, I'm wrestling with my own wants and desires. I long to be free of writing this book. I joke that writing books gives me PTSD. I tell myself I can afford to pay the publisher back the meager book advance I was given. I dream of sitting by a beach somewhere and protecting myself from the future pain of possible failure. I shouldn't admit that I expect the book to fail, but it's the truth. In my defense, my expectations are based on my past experiences. I've already written three books and became more disillusioned with God with each one. I had expected God to grant me success in writing. I had expected Him to allow me to have a bigger impact on others. I had expected the process to be smoother. So, when I was offered a chance to write another book, I leaned into my calling, but my desire has been mixed at best, and my expectations have been painfully negative.

But let's dig a little deeper for the truth. It's not freedom and a beach vacation that I desire the most. It's not even freedom from writing that I long for. What my heart truly desires is *success*. My expectations are based on a very specific desired outcome of success. I don't just want to write books. I want to write books that are bestsellers. Are these expectations God-given? I don't know. But the best way to know if my expectations are good or evil is to study what happens in my mind and heart when my expectations *aren't* met.

For me, my expectations nearly destroyed my faith. I wanted to succeed so much that my faith nearly shattered with the assumption that God was holding back from me what I thought would bring me happiness. That desire for success goes even deeper. It's not merely about selling a lot of books, but about my identity. I long to be seen as successful. I desire the security of success. I want peace that is rooted in my own ability to do well as opposed to receiving peace from God who has secured my worth and my peace in Christ. When God didn't do what I wanted Him to do for me, when God didn't meet my expectations for success, I almost abandoned Him. At the very least, I tried hiding from Him, like Eve in the garden.

But how can anyone hide from goodness and light? Ask Eve how well that worked out for her. It took one bite into the fruit for Adam and Eve to realize the hugeness of their loss. They tried to hide. They held their breath as God walked through the garden looking for them. But eventually, His light was too compelling to ignore. Eventually, it was God's goodness that won them back.

## Unearthing Our Deepest Longings

*All of our desires become idolatrous when we distort the character of God in our seeking to fulfill them.* All of our desires become sinful when they discredit the goodness of God in our lives.

Let me offer another example. Maybe your desire is for marriage. You long for it during years of singleness. You follow the rules you were taught about morality and faithfulness. You expect that doing the right thing will result in God providing you with a perfect mate. You pray and you wait. When it doesn't happen, you feel disappointed, and that disappointment festers.

You start to silently wonder about the goodness of God in your life. You're too afraid or ashamed to ask anyone about it. You wonder if it makes you sound desperate to do so. Soon you become disillusioned with God. Your faith starts eroding but you ignore it until you wake up one day and realize you're not sure you believe in God any longer.

But perhaps you've missed the real desire in your heart as you've focused on your longing for marriage. Every human has a God-given longing for intimacy. It's a longing that is meant to be filled not by a spouse but by God Himself. Hordes of married people will tell you of their post-honeymoon disappointment and the discovery that the person they married failed to meet their heart's deepest longings. Our culture has convinced us to believe that our future happiness depends on whether we find "the one." But God's purpose for our intimacy is deeper. Sadly, most of us have formed our desires not by what God's Word promises, but based on perceived cultural ideas. We were made for more. Spouses were never meant to meet our deepest longings. Only God can. Even if marriage never happens for you, your longing for intimacy is assured in Christ. Your desire for intimacy is forever secured in Christ.

Maybe your desire is to go to graduate school. You've worked so hard for it and prayed about it. Despite all your best efforts the door to your dream has closed. At first, you cut God some slack. You put a bandage on your wound and hoped for a better outcome next time. You even made excuses for God. But one day, you wake up in a career you hate, and find yourself crushed by the weight of your dead dreams. You take it out on God. He's the reason you're unhappy. He could have helped make your dream a reality but He didn't. By that point, it's easier to run from Him than to trust Him with your broken heart.

God's plan has never been for us to hide our desires from Him. He's never asked us to ignore our desires. On the contrary, God puts our desires in our hearts for a reason. God Himself is the dream-giver and the dream-maker. His relationship with humans starts with His promise to fulfill Abraham's desire for a son, and later Joseph's desire for his dream, and much later Moses's desire for his calling. God puts in each of our hearts the desire to be kind and to help others. God places in our souls a longing for *more*, a desire for harmony and success and unity with other people. God wires us to desire comfort and security. God even puts in us a longing for perfection.

Ah, that longing for perfection.

Ever since that day in Eden, when Adam and Eve blew it and were escorted out of perfect Eden, we've been wired for perfection. It's a longing for something better, something more. That "more" that we crave is our heart's longing for God. Every one of us is plagued with a restlessness that can only be filled by God.

Most of us have wrestled with feelings of disappointment in our Christian life. We live with the notion that if I do my part, God should do His. Instead of rightfully developing a healthy understanding of who God is, we've developed a Christian model where I am the center of my world and God is a puppet, waiting at my beck and call to fulfill my every whim.

We can tell the depth of the lie we've embraced by the level of disappointment we experience in our lives. For me, the lie seeped deep into my soul and it has taken God decades to dismantle it. But if I've learned anything about God in this lifetime, it's that He won't let His children believe lies about Him. He's a God of truth and that truth includes the truth about who He is, and who we are, and what He expects for us in this lifetime.

> **The biggest mistake we make in Christianity is to make ourselves the center of our story.**

*The biggest mistake we make in Christianity is to make ourselves the center of our story.* When we limit our longings to our own personal success stories, we limit perfection, beauty, and harmony. When we limit our desires to our own understanding, we miss out.

That perfection that we long for is ultimately found in only one place: the person of Jesus Christ. All of our God-given desires are ultimately met in Jesus Christ. Our desire for intimacy and healing and freedom and shamelessness, our desire for security and provision and perfection, are only met in Christ.

## Meanwhile, Back at the Ranch

In the months after I left my church, my Christian world started crumbling. The losses came fast and hard, and lost relationships were the hardest to replace. Friends I had counted on now saw me as divisive. Women I had poured my life into were no longer around. And what platform I did have had just been disrupted. The sales of my books suffered. The trajectory of my Christian speaking career took a punch. My dreams were shattered.

But worst of all, my belief in the goodness of God took a hit.

Disappointment has a way of undermining the goodness of God in your heart if you're not careful. Disappointment has a way of squelching hope, and hope is based on trust—trust that God in His goodness will come through for us.

*It's not supposed to be this way.* Like a song on repeat, that sentence looms in our souls, coloring our perspective, poisoning our hearts.

Our perspective becomes obscured when we base the goodness of God on the outcomes we desire. If God gives me what I want, then He must be good; and if God holds back, then He can't be trusted.

But there is a better way.

One of my favorite Bible characters is Peter. I like him because he's flawed like me. He talked a big game. Yet he publicly lived through one of the most devastating failures of all times, and God still used him for good.

Peter once made a bold claim: "Though they all fall away because of you, I will never fall away" (Matt. 26:33). A few pages in the story later, on the night of the crucifixion, he did the opposite. In fact, he did exactly what Jesus had warned he would do. He denied Jesus three times even before the rooster crowed once. I've always felt that one of the saddest verses in all of Scripture is Luke 22:62. After the Lord looks at Peter in his failure, Peter "went out and wept bitterly."

Peter was devastated. So much so that he almost quit. His faith was almost deconstructed. His steps faltered. Instead of gathering with the disciples to pray and share the good news of the gospel, he found his old boat and settled for the familiar. Peter's confidence in himself was shattered. It's easy to see why he wanted to quit.

*What good am I for now?*
*Why would God ever use me again?*

*Why even bother?*
*How could I even imagine that God had a plan for my life?*
*I'm just a failure. I might as well spend the rest of my days*
    *with the fish.*
*I can't believe I even tried.*

We've all been there. We've all felt the sting of disappointment, and we've wanted to hide.

Hardly anything is more difficult than coming face-to-face with the truth of who we are. It's one thing to tell the story of our pain and feel validated by it, but it's a whole other story to confess when we've been wrong. We spend our lives convinced that we are good enough, that God is lucky to have us, until things go wrong and we find ourselves squirming under the steady gaze of a Savior hanging on a cross for us. *The truth always has a way of coming out under the loving scrutiny of our Savior.*

Most people would reassure you at this point, telling you that you are indeed good enough, and that you can do it if you'll just try it differently this time. Most well-intentioned self-help gurus give you a list of ways to love yourself more and live your true authentic self. It might work for a while, but it will leave you utterly exhausted. No matter what we tell ourselves, our human potential to fill our deepest longings is limited. We might find a way to get married and have children; we might find a way to write a bestselling book and get into grad school, but eventually, our longings lead to expectations which lead to disappointment if not fully understood and aligned with God's purposes.

We must learn to see that God uses our disappointments to re-align and reorder our lives. *God uses our desires and unmet expectations, not to put a wedge in our relationship with Him but to deepen our communion and intimacy with Him.*

## Found

It was in the boat that Jesus found Peter. It wasn't at church or in a prayer meeting. It was out at sea in Peter's place of comfort, while Peter was coming to terms with yet another failure, a night spent without catching a single fish. But instead of judgment, Jesus met Peter with grace. Instead of anger, Jesus came to Peter and showed him love. Jesus helped him make a big catch, and then Jesus cooked Peter breakfast.

What kind of Savior does that? What kind of Savior loves like that?

*It's not supposed to be this way.* That's true. Life in God's plan is not supposed to be painful and hard and hurtful. God created us in a perfect world with everything we needed for joy and fulfillment. He created us for unhindered communion with Him and intimacy with Him. God created us for love. But our sins blew it for us; we, like those before us, end up falling for the same lies, over and over. Negative, unhelpful messages swirl in our minds:

> *If God really loved you, He'd give you what you want.*
> *You can't trust God with the things that matter most to you.*
> *God knows that you could be happy if you could just have that one thing.*

The good news of the gospel is that, even in our failure, God is still waiting with open arms for us. He waited in the garden for Adam and Eve. He called them out of hiding. He clothed their nakedness with the animal skins, and He renewed His promise to them. He gave them a way to meet their deepest longings: He promised them Himself. The only way to happiness is to come to God with your longings and trust Him to meet you there.

Like Adam and Eve and so many before me, I chose to hide from

God in my failure and disappointment. I stopped going to church; I hid wherever I could. I didn't count on the fact that you can't hide from God. He has a way of finding us even when we don't want to be found.

You might be hiding in your own disappointment right now. Your life is not what you expected it to be. You hoped that God would step in and give you your own future and hope (Jer. 29:11). You banked on "all things work[ing] together for good" (Rom. 8:28), but instead, you've gotten nothing but closed doors and a broken heart. It wasn't supposed to be this way.

You're right. Life isn't supposed to hurt like it does. Children aren't supposed to die. Families aren't supposed to be displaced and murdered. Women aren't supposed to be raped and sold into slavery. That's why Jesus came to earth. That's why Jesus died. He came to make wrong right. He came to meet our deepest longings. He came to fulfill our expectations. He came to give us more than we could ever imagine. He's the only one who can satisfy us completely.

The magic of God—if I can be so bold to use that phrase—is that He has a way of finding us in our disappointment and calming our hearts with His love. He did it in a garden once, and He did it by a seashore. And He'll do it again when you least expect Him to. He'll do it even after you've counted yourself out of the story.

Most of us spend so much time asking the question, "Why did my story end up this way?" Why not let your disappointment form you for a change? Why not redefine your expectations based on your heart's true longings?

This chapter might feel esoteric, so let me make it as practical as I can as we come to the end of it. The way to let your disappointments shape your faith is by stopping yourself every time you feel like your life wasn't *supposed* to turn out this way and asking yourself these questions:

*Why am I disappointed right now?*
*What did I really desire and long for?*
*Is that desire good or bad?*
*If that desire is good, can I surrender it to God who is good*
*and trust Him with the outcome?*
*If that desire is bad, am I willing to let it go?*

Most of the time our problem is that we haven't taken into account the fact that our story is not over yet. God might just be getting started with you. Your present disappointment might just be the building block to your God-given destiny.

Won't you come out of hiding? You have no reason to be ashamed anymore. You are deeply loved. You are seen. You belong. You can let go of your version of Christianity that is steeped in unmet expectations and unfulfilled longings. It's time to bring your longings to the Savior who is waiting for you with open arms, whispering, *welcome home.*

**SPEND A FEW MINUTES CONSIDERING THESE QUESTIONS,**
**and bring your thoughts and feelings to God in prayer:**

*Do you relate to the story of Peter? Which part feels most familiar to you?*

*What are some of the disappointments you have experienced?*

*Can you hand over your expectations, desires, and disappointments to God now? If not, what's holding you back?*

*Chapter 3*

# WHY CAN'T I OVERCOME SIN IN MY LIFE?

We had just walked into my house when one of my nephews, who shall remain unnamed, approached me in the kitchen and asked me to come into the family room.

"Something's happened to the leather chair, Lina."

I walked the few steps to the chair and noticed it was scratched up in four distinctly linear places. It looked horrible.

"How did that happen?" I asked.

"I don't know. I was just walking by and saw it."

If you're a mother, then you've probably already assumed that my nephew was guilty until proven innocent. But I'm the aunt, and we had barely been home for five minutes, so I grabbed the phone, baffled by the sudden onset of the scratches, and wondered if I had worn something with a sharp object on it when I last sat on the chair.

I called the furniture store where I bought it and explained my problem, insinuating no less that the chair was defective and that I would not be appeased until they did something about it. After going back and forth for some time, the person on the phone gave me a couple of tricks to try and fix it, which I sheepishly admit did work, and then successfully sold me a leather cleaner over the phone. I went to grab my wallet and realized it was out in my car. I told the lady I'd need a minute, walked out to the car and grabbed my wallet.

I was missing for no more than twenty seconds when I walked back in, noticed my nephew a few feet from the chair and glanced toward the chair.

Instead of four fading marks, I could now clearly see fifteen distinctly linear scratches on the chair. I couldn't believe it. I interrupted the lady who was still on the phone and expressed my dismay.

"This chair is demon-possessed," I exclaimed. I literally turned my back for twenty seconds and now it's full of scratches. I was upset. I let her know. I made no apology for my frustration and when she insinuated that my innocent nephew might have been the cause of the scratches, I repudiated her theory with vengeance.

She told me to hold on while she got a manager to talk to me.

I waited.

And then I glanced at my nephew, and some supernatural force gently dropped a new idea in my head: Could he possibly have damaged the chair? Could it be possible, that despite his calm demeanor, he was lying to my face?

I imagine you know the outcome of that story. It took about four hours of my sister's persuasive parenting skills to bring out the truth. My nephew had indeed scratched the chair not once but several times—willfully. When asked why he had done it, his tearful response was a timid, "I don't know."

Like all of us, this boy needed transformation.

A couple of weeks later I was at my sister's house for dinner. I asked her how my nephew was doing. He was doing okay, she said, but had told her in their evening devotions that he didn't think God heard his prayers. When she asked him why, he answered that he keeps asking God to change him, but nothing was happening.

At age six, he is having a crisis of faith. He doesn't understand why he can't overcome the sin in his life, and why God isn't doing His part to help him change.

I empathize. I've spent a lot of my Christian years there, and it's the most discouraging place in the world. So many Christians are stuck in a cycle of defeated living, experiencing no lasting victory over sin, and the result is a disbelief in the power of God to transform us. Without power for victorious living, faith in God is ultimately questioned and doubt soon takes over. Even worse is the price that shame places on us. Because of our shame, most of us gloss over any deep admission of sin in church groups. We sit in small group meetings and speak in generalities, giving just enough information to look sensible but never getting to the heart of the matter. We finish our small group meetings and rush out, telling ourselves we've dealt with our issues, but we go home alone, isolated in our confusion, and far from transformed. The longer we walk in Christ, the deeper our shame becomes, and the wider the gap from God grows.

What's behind our sinful patterns? Why does an all-powerful God seem powerless to change us? Or are *we* the problem? We're tempted to conclude that just because we're not changing, God is powerless to change us. But if God does exist, and we're not changing, then we've got to figure out why. Why does sin have such a hold on us? Why is it that others seem to cruise where we only sputter? Like my nephew, I've struggled to get to the root of why I consistently and knowingly choose to hurt others and myself even when I know better. Like him, I've wanted to change. I've felt stuck in a cycle of shame and defeat.

Most of us can write sermons on what the Bible says about sin and what our pastor has taught us about sin. Yet most of us still struggle with the problem of sin. No wonder we feel like quitting. No wonder we've got questions!

But what's truly behind our struggle to change?

## Besetting Sins, Bad Habits, or Addictions

When it comes to overcoming habitual sin in the Christian's life, it's important to clarify some distinctions. The Bible teaches us that we're all born sinners. The moment we come to Christ we're given a new nature. We've exchanged our sin for Christ's perfect righteousness. God tells us that, in principle, we're no longer slaves to sin. Yet, truth be told, most Christians live like we're slaves to something. Is it bad habits that we can't break? Habits of anger, habits of addiction, habits of gossip? Or do most Christians struggle with addictions that are impossible to overcome?

Now that I am well into my middle-aged years, I have come to understand that many Christians have patterns of sin that will follow us through our lives. There are some things in my life that I struggled with in my teens and that continue to ensnare me today. It's frustrating. It's infuriating. The author of Hebrews calls these patterns sins that "so easily beset us" (Heb. 12:1 KJV). These are sins that we continuously struggle with and have a weakness toward. They are sins that entangle us. These are sins that expose our vulnerabilities and threaten to destroy our faith in a God whose very promise is to transform us into His likeness.

These besetting sins can feel like addictions. They can seem like bad habits. But no matter what name you give them, they can and must be overcome.

You might be addicted to lying or to drugs. You might be addicted to impatience or to sex. You might be addicted to gluttony or stealing, to jealousy or alcohol, or to your ministry or your work. The list is long.

### Sin's Lie Is Powerful

Besetting sin can be a lot like a thorn in the flesh. It is powerful and persistent in its attack on us. In 2 Corinthians 12:7–9, the apostle Paul made reference to a thorn in his flesh that harassed him and made him feel weak. Christians have long tried to guess what Paul's thorn in the flesh was. Despite our not knowing, most of us readily identify with Paul's illustration. We each have our own thorn in the flesh.

Let's say that my thorn in the flesh is eating marshmallows. (Don't get stuck on the illustration.) I love marshmallows like most people do, but if you follow the logic of the illustration, I believe it will help you understand how powerful sin's lie can be.

As far back as I can remember, I've been hooked on eating marshmallows (again, this is just an illustration). I eat marshmallows not because I'm not sure whether God approves of it, but despite knowing He does not. That's how sin works. We don't sin because we're not sure sin is wrong, but despite knowing it's wrong. Sin is an act of rebellion against God. At the heart of sin is a raging battle: my will or God's.

The problem with marshmallows is that they are enticing. When I look at a marshmallow, I lose sight of God. I've tried to convince myself that I can both think about God and marshmallows at the same time, but years into eating marshmallows I know better: it's always either God or marshmallows. Yet, I keep a bag of marshmallows in my pantry promising myself not to eat them; but who am I kidding? They have too much power over me.

> **We don't sin because we're not sure sin is wrong, but despite knowing it's wrong.**

I eat marshmallows when I'm sad. I eat marshmallows when I'm bored. I eat marshmallows when God feels far away. I eat marshmallows when I'm tired of doing all the right things. And truthfully, sometimes I eat marshmallows just because I want to.

Every single time I eat marshmallows, I feel bad about it. Somewhere between the moment that I start thinking about marshmallows to the point of no return, I lose the urge to fight. The promise marshmallows make becomes deafening. They whisper to me, "We will make you happy." And you know how this story goes: one marshmallow is never enough. So, I lie to myself: *God won't care if I eat one marshmallow. No one will know if I eat a marshmallow. It's just one marshmallow; it's not like I'm eating a whole s'more. I'll stop eating marshmallows tomorrow. So what? Some people don't even think eating marshmallows is a sin. I just grew up in the wrong denomination. Don't spiritualize this. Everyone gets hungry from time to time. It's normal to eat marshmallows.*

Sadly, the minute I give in and eat the marshmallow, I see clearly. I hate marshmallows. They make me feel sick and ashamed and weak. They never bring me the happiness they promised.

So, I do what we all would do: I confess my sin to God. I tell Him I'm sorry. I tell Him I hate marshmallows. I'll never eat another marshmallow again.

I want it to be true. I throw away the bag of marshmallows and promise myself and God that I'll never do it again. Until one day, I accidentally walk past a bag of marshmallows at the grocery store. And I remember how much I love marshmallows. I remember how hard of a week I've had. I tell myself I deserve a marshmallow. So, I buy the bag of marshmallows telling myself that this time it won't hurt me. I can control this whole marshmallow thing.

Then I eat the marshmallows.

The minute I eat, I see. I hate marshmallows. They make me sad. They make me feel weak and ashamed and lonely and unloved.

By that point I can't keep track of how many times I've told God how much I hate marshmallows and prefer Him instead. I can't keep track of how many times I've promised Him I won't do it again. Will He believe me this time? Will my resolve stick this time? Who am I kidding? God must see right through me: I still don't hate marshmallows enough to stop buying them. So why am I even bothering?

Now the real questions start: Do I even *know* God? Am I even a Christian? Christians *ought* to hate marshmallows. Christians don't stay stuck in a marshmallow-eating world. And even if I was a Christian, why would God even want me now? I'm a fraud and a liar. I guess I might as well just enjoy the marshmallows. I'm a lost cause anyway. And I'm tired—so tired. I don't want to fight this battle anymore. I want to quit.

Do you feel stuck in a similar cycle? It's the worst place in the world. It's been said that "sin will take you farther than you want to go, keep you longer than you want to stay, and cost you more than you want to pay."[1] But it's more than that. For some of us, this pattern of defeat is the near deconstruction of our faith. The idea that God promises to transform people but hasn't bothered to transform *me* is too much to bear.

Sin will blind you to the truth while promising to satisfy you. Sin will ravage your soul while promising to relieve your pain. Sin always promises what it cannot provide and delivers what you do not desire.

We're not the first people to struggle with sin. Have you ever stopped to consider that almost every man or woman that God ever used greatly struggled with sin?

> *Abraham struggled with fear.*
> *Sarah couldn't shake her doubt.*
> *Jacob was a liar.*
> *Judah slept with his daughter-in-law.*
> *Moses had an anger problem.*

*Aaron was an idol worshiper.*
*Samson was a womanizer.*
*Jonah was a racist.*
*Peter struggled with pride.*

The list is long, but God's track record is clear. He doesn't use us based on our performance but because of His love for us. God is a covenant God. He never breaks His promises. When He called Abraham, He made a covenant with him where He swore to remain faithful to him no matter what (Gen. 12). In the New Testament, God established a new covenant with His people through Jesus Christ. His death on the cross secured our relationship with Him once and for all. God goes to great lengths to save us, not because of who we are but despite our weaknesses, failings, and even sins. The whole thing hinges on His grace.

### Grace Changes Everything

I was sixteen years old when I first encountered God's grace. Having moved from Beirut, Lebanon, to Green Bay, Wisconsin, the year before, my parents sent me off to Christian camp for the summer. Something happened to me one night after the preacher said, "Amen." I don't remember what he talked about, but when he asked us to go outside and spend time with God, I knew my heart was changed forever. I could feel God's presence with me as I gazed into the star-filled Wisconsin sky. I was touched deeply in my heart with a peace that I can't articulate. That day changed the course of my life. I wasn't thinking about marshmallows that day. Only God would do for me.

That day I received God's love for me without question. I was loved by the Almighty and no one could convince me otherwise. Tim Keller has written, "The gospel is this: We are more sinful and flawed in ourselves than we ever dared believe, yet at the very same time we are more loved and accepted in Jesus Christ than we ever dared hope."[2] God knew me so well and still loved me so much. I knew that to be true on that beautiful night in Wisconsin. But my memory grew dim over time.

What is it that makes us forget God's goodness and grace when we're grappling with our addictions and vices? We forget the same things others have forgotten before us. We forget that at the root of our battle with sin is a struggle over longing. We long for what God hasn't provided. We wait and we persevere, and when it becomes too much, we take matters into our own hands. We choose the temporary satisfaction of our desires over God's faithfulness later on. We choose satisfaction our way over satisfaction God's way. We choose to control the outcome of our own happiness. We choose and we fail over and over again.

We choose to not believe in the goodness of God and step in to take the reins of our own lives. If God won't give us the happiness we want, we'll find a way to get it ourselves. Sin at its most basic form is a failure to trust God. *Sin is less about your hormones or your genetic makeup and more about your view of God.* As long as you see God holding back what you think you need most, you will never find the power to overcome the sin in your life. The key is in trusting that He knows what you need the most.

### A Fight We Must Win

The battle over sin is a battle of desire. John Piper says this about sin:

> I'll tell you why you sin: because sin makes promises to you, and you believe them. . . . Sin promises . . . "What I have to offer is better, more satisfying, more enjoyable, more hope-giving than Christ." . . . Sin promises to be better, longer, deeper, sweeter, more satisfying. And to the degree that we are deceived by those

promises, we sin. Nobody sins out of duty . . . We sin out of pleasure-seeking. And the only reason we opt for a sinful action is because the devil and our own nature has promised us that action will produce pleasure, satisfaction, fame.[3]

Sin promises something better, but it never delivers. Sin promises to exceed our expectations, knowing that behind every expectation is a heart that wants more. Our problem is that even when we think we know what we want, we don't see what we need.

You're stuck in a life that you don't want. You're stuck in a job you don't like. You're stuck in a marriage that isn't what you hoped it would be. You're stuck in a ministry that you're starting to resent. You're stuck under church leadership you don't respect. You're stuck in your singleness. You're stuck in financial debt you can't get out of. You're stuck with results you didn't expect. You're stuck with a weight you hate.

Sin promises to give you a moment of pleasure in a world full of pain. Sin promises to satisfy your anger for a moment, to soothe your ache for a second, to relieve your anxieties by distracting you from your present. We sin because we don't like the life we have and are too afraid to admit it to God. Sometimes we sin because we're angry at God, frustrated at His pace, annoyed with the way He's treating us. We sin because we stop believing the goodness of God.

*Sin is not a habit issue. It's a heart issue. Sin is not about behavior modification but desire modification.*

The big question becomes: How do we change our desires?

### The Catalyst for Change

Though there are many things that can lead us to sin, much of our struggle with sin is rooted in our not trusting in the goodness of God. We must get to the root of why we don't trust the goodness of God.

The answer lies in our desires. We come to God with our desires, but we often leave disappointed. When we're hurting, we expect God to remove our suffering and fix our problems. We miss that delays and suffering have a purpose. We become blinded by what we want. When our desires supersede our view of the goodness of God, sin moves in.

It's a tale as old as time. We've already heard the story of Eve who doubted God's goodness and chose what she wanted. Her sin spilled over to her son Cain who desired acceptance but wanted it on his own terms. Lot longed for the good life and settled in lush Sodom and Gomorrah. Esau hungered for the blessing he'd given up and almost murdered his brother because of it. We see a repetitive pattern of blinding desire leading to sin and eventual death.

The prodigal son had the same problem. He longed for his freedom. He desired his independence. He got sick of his father's ways and wanted to do things on his own. So he took what he could and he split. It didn't take long for him to realize that life outside of the protection of the father is never as good as we expect it to be.

It was only when the prodigal reached the end of his rope that he finally came to his senses. He had to reach rock bottom before he was finally willing to look up.

What has made you doubt the goodness of God in your life? What has made you choose to numb your pain with what you think will satisfy you? It's hard to see God's presence when you're focused on your pain. We forget that God sometimes allows what He hates to accomplish what He loves. When we're hurting and God doesn't step in to stop our pain, it's easy to question God's goodness. In those seasons, we barely remember our way back home.

But home is where we need to go if we have any hope of making it.

### The Way Back Home

The prodigal had to make it all the way to the pigsty before longing for home again.

The same happened to Samson in the Old Testament. He made it his lifestyle to sin. Though he had been chosen by God for a life of anointed service, he made bad choices over and over and over again. Despite knowing God, he chose his own pleasure over God repeatedly. He loved his "marshmallows" and was stuck in a cycle of sin and defeat. His parents tried to point out the truth. Eventually, desire for what he wanted won the battle. A woman named Delilah brought him to his knees and he lost everything. His eyes were plucked out, ensuring he would never see another woman again. His only visual memories were his mistakes and his regrets. He was chained to a plow and spent his days blindly walking around a mill.

It was only when Samson lost his eyes that he finally got his vision back. Somewhere in the pit he came to find out that even in our darkest spaces, God's presence is still right there. On that day Samson's only hope was that the same God who had called him and loved him in his youth still loved him in his brokenness. So he hedged his bets on God and he prayed. Samson finally understood that no amount of self-satisfaction or self-actualization would replace the joy that comes from living humbly and honestly in the presence of the Lord.

Samson's life shows us that *it's not the strength of our repentance that earns us our forgiveness but the goodness of our God.* Samson never lived a day past his repentance, yet his name made it onto the list of men who lived by faith in Hebrews 11.

The prodigal experienced God's goodness in similar fashion. After coming to his senses, he understood that life in his father's house was better than life alone in a pigsty. He had tried to find his satisfaction away from home. He had tried to find himself away from his father's house. But the very things that the prodigal was hoping would fulfill his longings failed him. When he reached bottom, his heart was still tethered to his father's heart.

He then slowly made his way back home. Burdened with questions about his own self-worth, filled with insecurities about how he would be received, the last thing the prodigal expected was his father's arms wide open. Yet that's exactly what he found. The last thing the son expected was for the father to be running towards him. This wasn't just forgiveness, this was overflowing, unconditional, steadfast love that had never given up on his son.

*This* is the heart of our Father.

### Finding a Superior Pleasure

I'm no longer a "There's a Three-Step Process to Living a Victorious Christian Life" kind of person. I've been there, and I've tried that. While it may soothe your Enneagram type to get a list of to-dos and cross it off slowly, trying to overcome sin by sheer willpower and a good three-step plan has not worked for me. It only creates in us a spirit of self-righteousness and exhaustion. Eventually, we see God as a stern task master, causing us to drift even further away from His presence.

Sheer willpower is also no answer for our sin problem. Willful determination is no solution for the disillusioned Christian. It will take much more than yourself to overcome sin and find the joy that's promised to you in Christ.

How does Jesus become better than anything else in our world again? You and I know where to find this superior pleasure: we met Him the moment we gave our lives to God. We've experienced this joy before. His name is Jesus, and He's the only all-satisfying treasure.

We simply have to find our way back home to the arms of our Savior.

## Burning Marshmallows

For years I wrestled with God and kept settling for my own version of "marshmallows." Anytime I didn't like the path God had for me, I found solace in my bag of marshmallows.

When I left my church, my Christian world imploded. My community blew up. My accountability system evaporated. My whole life structure fell apart. And slowly my faith in God drifted.

I started eating marshmallows to numb myself. Then one day, instead of a marshmallow, I grabbed for a "s'more." A s'more, to follow the illustration, is a marshmallow on steroids. The minute I ate the s'more I knew I'd crossed a line I never thought I would. In that moment I saw who I really was. I had never imagined that I was the kind of person who would ever eat s'mores, but there it was, this version of myself. I knew I had finally landed in the pigsty.

It was a wake-up call for me. It was a moment of decision. Would I surrender what I thought I needed to be happy for the riches I'd already been so freely given?

Surrender is a familiar Christian word. You might have heard it at camp or at a revival meeting. Surrender is a word that might elicit a whole array of emotions in your heart. But in its truest form, surrender is the biggest win we will ever achieve. One of the biggest mistakes we make is to think of surrender as a giving up of what we want, when in reality it is a letting go. *When we surrender what we think we need to be happy in exchange for God, we're not settling for less, we're settling for more.*

> **When we surrender what we think we need to be happy in exchange for God, we're not settling for less, we're settling for more.**

Surrender to God is indeed our biggest win.

Surrender is what eventually moves us from the pigsty to the palace. Surrender hinges on accepting and receiving the goodness of God in our life. Surrender starts in our will but soon moves to our heart. Surrender is nudged by the Holy Spirit of God who already lives in the heart of every follower of Jesus. For some of us it takes hitting rock bottom before we become sensitive enough and tender-hearted enough to heed what the Holy Spirit has been trying to do all along.

What we find the moment we surrender is a Father waiting for us with open arms ready to welcome us back home. That is my story.

### From Duty to Delight

I've been a critic of Christian systems since I left my old church. Religious systems can be used to control us and alienate us from the very place they're supposed to lead us. Yet God in His love has used the same practices and disciplines that I was familiar with to bring me back to His heart. In the book of the Revelation, Jesus calls His church to go back to first things in an effort to recapture its first love for Him: The Word of God. Prayer. Community. The Eucharist.

When I reckoned that I was in the pigsty, I reached out for community. I called a friend who had been in the pigsty before. She helped pull me out of the pit. I went back to church. I started going to small group again. I recommitted to spending more time alone with God. I dug up my old practices and infused them with a new rhythm of delight. I stopped blaming the methods for the outcomes I had experienced and found that once I'd let go of my stockpile of marshmallows, I had room in my heart for delight.

I felt I was being born again . . . again, and it had nothing to do with my willpower and everything to do with God's steadfast goodness and unconditional love toward me.

My desire for Jesus grew—slowly at first, and then fast. I remembered that night at camp back when I was sixteen. I blew the dust off old memories with God and started feeling His presence again. I felt joy again. It was a new beginning.

I still fight the battle over sinful desires. When sinful desires threaten to take over, I reorient my heart again to Jesus. I make room for the Spirit's prompting. I pray a whispered prayer: *Lord, open my eyes that I may see You, open my ears that I may hear You, open my mouth that I may praise You, and open my heart to receive all You have for me today.*

This kind of work takes solitude and silence. This kind of work is slow work. Most of us are not accustomed to any process that takes time, but life in Christ is a journey that unfolds one step at a time.

I'm not oblivious to the challenges that still lie ahead. I know I'll see a marshmallow one day and look longingly at it. When that happens, I won't beat myself on the head over it. It will just be a reminder to me that I am made for more. It will be a reminder that marshmallows will never satisfy me. Only Jesus will.

If you're stuck in a cycle of sin that has caused you to doubt whether you even know God, you're not alone. If you've resigned yourself to failure, you're not alone. If you're stuck in a cycle of sin that has caused you to wonder whether Christianity is true, you're not alone. A famous pastor recently admitted that his faith was deconstructed because of the sin in his life. Given a choice between victory over sin or a lifetime of sin, he chose sin and discounted his Christianity. His inability to overcome sin reflected his belief that the promise of his sin would bring him greater joy than the promise of the Son. He believed sin's lie that promises that sin is better than Jesus.

Repentance matters. Surrender matters. Even our desires matter, especially when we allow God to shape those desires in His goodness. As Christians we might understand that victory is ours in Christ, and we might even believe it. What needs growth is our ability to live it out in the power of the Holy Spirit. But *the thing that draws us out of the pit and into the palace again is God's love.* God's covenantal, unconditional, steadfast love will never fail us, even when we're too far away to feel it. You might feel like you're past the point of return. You couldn't be more wrong.

Jeremiah 31:2–4 says:

> "The people who survived the sword
>    found grace in the wilderness;
> when Israel sought for rest,
>    the Lord appeared to him from far away.
> I have loved you with an everlasting love;
>    therefore, I have continued my faithfulness to you.
> Again I will build you, and you shall be built,
>    O virgin Israel!
> Again you shall adorn yourself with tambourines
>    and shall go forth in the dance of the merrymakers."

This is grace—that we are loved though undeserving. That we are offered hope and joy where we deserve punishment and shame. Jesus paid the price; all to Him we owe. He paid the price for every single marshmallow you and I have ever eaten or will ever eat again.

Now receive His love and live.

**SPEND A FEW MINUTES CONSIDERING THESE QUESTIONS,**
**and bring your thoughts and feelings to God in prayer:**

*Are there unhealthy habits or addictions that you run to when you are hurting?*

*In what ways has sin kept you from experiencing God's love?*

*Can you thank God for His grace and His embrace, despite your sins and shortcomings, now?*

# Chapter 4

# IS THIS HOW CHRISTIANS ARE SUPPOSED TO ACT?

Twice in my life I've felt rejected by God, and both times it had to do with His people.

The first time I was young and idealistic. I had fallen in love with my best friend of ten years but was too foolish to realize it. We had been inseparable since the day we met in our freshman year at our Christian college. We were both pre-med. I thought he was in love with me, but I kept pushing him back, too young and naïve to see what was right there before my eyes. It took me getting engaged to a different guy and making it all the way until two weeks before the wedding to finally wake up from my stupor.

I refused to walk down the aisle with the wrong guy. But because I was a woman of my word, I couldn't break off the engagement without a sign from God. So, I looked for a sign. I prayed for a sign. Then I went for a run. It was a hot and humid day in Houston, Texas, and before my head hit the pillow that night, I had found a verse that matched my need in that moment and called it a sign.

I circled the verse and wrote a note to myself reassuring my now fragile heart that God always works everything out for good for His children. The next day, I ended my engagement.

Then I waited for God to make the next move.

And I waited.

I got tired of waiting, so I took matters into my own hands. I sat down with the man I thought was my soulmate and admitted my feelings to him. I assumed he'd gotten the same memo from God, but tragically, something had shifted in his heart after I had said yes to another man's proposal. He was no longer interested.

Still, I believed God for His promises and kept on waiting. I believed that God would give me the miracle of a perfect love story despite the big mess I'd managed to make.

A year later, God still hadn't shown up for me in the way I wanted Him to. I was devastated. I moved to Jacksonville, Florida, for my pediatric ER fellowship because I didn't have a better plan. I hoped that starting out in a new city where I knew no one would help heal my pain.

It didn't. My best friend never came chasing after me. It hurt. Sometimes it still hurts.

I started my fellowship in a fog. I lived in denial by day and in despair by night. I hated the place I was in. I had no one to talk to about my pain. I was ashamed to admit that I had fallen in love with the same guy who I spent ten years telling everyone I would never marry. I was ashamed to admit that I had been rejected. I was ashamed to admit how lonely I was, how abandoned I felt, and how guilty I felt for what I assumed was my part in the demise of my love story.

In that season of my life I would come home to a lonely apartment after a long ER shift and sit on my couch in the living room feeling sorry for myself. My Bible lay open in the other room to the page where I had circled the verse with God's promise to me. Every time I looked at my Bible I felt the heavens smirking at me.

God felt very far away in that season of my life.

Several months passed. Eventually, my wound scabbed over. I never told a soul about my pain. In the decade that followed I resolved to get my act together and move on. I finished my fellowship and moved to Chicago. I told myself I was strong enough to handle the pain. I told myself the wound had healed.

Then six years ago, I left my church and everything came crashing down. I guess you could say the scab was unroofed and the bleeding was worse than I thought it would be.

By that point, I was convinced that God had a calling on my life to teach the Bible. While I still practiced medicine in the pediatric ER, my life had become the church. My community was the church. My friends were the church. When I left my church, my entire social structure was uprooted from me. In one fell swoop I'd lost my pastor, my close circle of friends, my Bible teaching ministry, which was so intricately tied to the life of my church, and my foreseeable future. I was devastated.

I then made the same mistake I made ten years earlier: I assumed God would fix my problem right then and there. Once again, the signs of God's presence were not as obvious as I wanted them to be. I became disillusioned with God, but I also reached a dangerous conclusion about God's people: Christians are not to be trusted. No matter how godly they seem to be, they will eventually hurt you.

In both the situation with my love interest and with my church, I had expected the Christians in my life to understand their part in my pain. They didn't. Instead, the Christian young man I had fallen in love with and the pastor I had so admired seemed to simply shake the dust off their sandals and move on, as far as I was concerned. I felt isolated, hurt, and confused.

I wish I could tell you that my two sorry tales were the only times I've been wounded by other Christians. They're not. Humans have an incredible capacity to hurt each other. The capacity to hurt one another does not automatically evaporate the moment one becomes a Christian. One of the hardest questions to answer when you've been hurt by God's people is: Why doesn't God step in and do something about it? Is there a reason why God allows us to go through the pain of being wounded by other Christians? Could Joseph's words in Genesis 50:20 indeed be true: "As for you, you meant evil against me, but God meant it for good"?

*Few things have hurt the cause of Christianity more than the pain inflicted on Christians by other Christians.* Ask most Christians who used to go to church why they don't go anymore, and they'll tell you: it's the Christians. An online search of the number one most common reason for leaving the church is not Jesus—it's His people.

Why do Christians hurt other Christians? Is it because they've been hurt before? Is it because they're unaware of the pain they're causing or are they just too distracted with their own agendas? Is it because the devil made them do it? While some inflicted pain is inadvertent, tragically, sometimes the pain against us is willful and repetitive. We might never know the exact reason why Christians hurt each other, but here's what I do know: this kind of pain is deep and some never recover from it. *I'm also convinced that God's purpose is to use these painful experiences with rejection and suffering to redirect our calling.*

If you think I sound like Pollyanna urging you to find your rainbow in every storm, please forgive me. I've actually always been much more an Eeyore than a Pollyanna. I specialize in worst-case scenarios. Even as I type these words, I deeply empathize with the pain you're feeling. You might be living with an abusive spouse who looks like a model citizen at the church deacon's meeting, then treats you with unfathomable cruelty when he's not at church. While this book is not about abuse, it's inevitable that I mention abuse in a #metoo and #churchtoo culture where supposedly respectable people do really hurtful and destructive things.

Or you might be working for a Christian boss who demands too much, speaks too harshly to you, and overlooks you regularly when it's time for a promotion or a raise. Your sense of rejection may be attached to your dreams. You've faced so many closed doors in ministry that the idea of church just makes you want to vomit. It's easy to become disillusioned by Christianity. You long for God to vindicate you. You've tried everything in your power to make the best of the present you're living in, but the stacks are persistently against you.

Your pain is justified. Yet this is not the end of your story. God is not against you. *His purpose for your life is not sabotaged by other people's sin or the way you've responded to them so far.* God is closer to you than you feel Him to be right now. His hand is still guiding your life.

> **God's purpose for your life is not sabotaged by other people's sin or the way you've responded to them.**

## Rejection and Its Effect

There was a man named Gideon who once thought God was against him. One day, Gideon was alone in a field feeling sorry for the pain he and his people were enduring. Life was unfair for the people of Israel in those days. They were under the oppression of the Midianites with no signs of God anywhere on the horizon. The people were hungry and their efforts to gather food were derailed by the heavy hand of their enemies.

One day, Gideon was beating out the wheat in the winepress hoping to quietly sneak out some food to feed his family. Gideon felt like a failure. He felt God had failed him. He couldn't see past the pain of his present circumstances. When the angel of the Lord appeared to him and promised He would use him to save Israel, Gideon laughed and said,

> "Please, my lord, if the LORD is with us, why then has all this happened to us? And where are all his wonderful deeds that our

fathers recounted to us, saying, 'Did not the LORD bring us up from Egypt?' But now the LORD has forsaken us and given us into the hand of Midian." (Judg. 6:13)

God was undeterred: "Go in this might of yours and save Israel from the hand of Midian; do not I send you?" (v. 14).

Gideon's response was priceless: "Please, Lord, how can I save Israel? Behold, my clan is the weakest in Manasseh, and I am the least in my father's house" (v. 15).

In Gideon's mind, the case was closed. God had allowed Gideon and the people of Israel to fail. Instead of stepping in and providing for them, God seemed to have abandoned them. Instead of keeping His promises, God seemed to have forgotten them. You could say Gideon felt God rejected him and his people.

I sympathize with Gideon. One of the biggest temptations I have to overcome when I'm dealing with rejection is the temptation to reach the wrong conclusions about God. I reach wrong conclusions about God's character and His purposes for me. I reach wrong conclusions about both my past and my future. I reach wrong conclusions about what God still longs to do in my life. Instead of letting the character of God lead my thinking toward peace, I allow my pain to mar my perception of the very character of God.

We're all tempted to reach the wrong conclusions when we're living under the weight of our pain. Pain has a way of distorting our perspectives, especially when it's the supposedly godly people in our lives who are inflicting the greatest pain on us. Why doesn't God step in and stop them? How could a good God let them get away with so much evil? But perhaps we judge God too soon. God's Word promises that in due time every wrong *will* be set right. In Ephesians 5:13, God promises us that "when anything is exposed by the light, it becomes visible." In 2 Corinthians 5:10, Paul wrote that "we must all appear before the judgment seat of Christ, so that each one may receive what is due for what he has done in the body, whether good or evil." It's in the waiting that we must remember who God really is. It's in the gap that our faith is tested.

Moses struggled with reaching the wrong conclusions about God during his four decades in the wilderness. Little by little, he got to the place where he was no longer convinced that God's power applied to him anymore. Forty years in the wilderness created a place for Moses to sink deep into hiding, where he became overwhelmed by his insecurities.

Rejection is hard no matter its source, but when rejection comes from unlikely places, it becomes almost impossible to breathe. Rejection by God's people blinds us to God's love. As a result, we become self-protective. We give in to the lie that God can't be trusted, that He might prefer "them" over "me" since they seem to be winning. We feel threatened, and when humans feel threatened, we choose one of two responses: we fight or we run. Initially, most of us might choose to fight. But fight after fight without a positive outcome leaves us exhausted. Fight after fight without reconciliation leaves us cynical. Fight after fight without restitution of relationship leaves us feeling vulnerable. So, we run. We isolate ourselves and hide, which sounds logical at first glance, until we lump God and the people who hurt us in the same category, eventually isolating ourselves even from God.

But there is a better way.

It's the way of faith. It's the way of God's love overruling our insecurities and our fears. It is God who finds us when we're hurting. It is God who looks for us on the backside of the wilderness and in the heat of the day while we're beating out wheat. It is God's goodness that always draws us out of hiding even when we don't see the need or have the desire to come out of hiding.

God is committed to reminding us of His goodness when we're hurting. He's committed to proving to us over and over again just how much we mean to Him. He's resolved to show us that every human life has value, including mine. It is God's sovereign goodness that calls us out of our painful places. It is His justice that steps in and vindicates us even after we've mentally assumed our story is over. And it is the power of God that allows us to step back into our own life and calling even after we've counted ourselves out.

He did it for Moses. He did it for Gideon. He did it for me, and He'll do it for you. Our wounds have a way of causing us to become more focused on what's happening to us than what God is trying to accomplish in us. But when you least expect it, God steps in and faithfully points the way forward.

## A Redirection

The year I left Houston for Jacksonville, my heart was broken and my future felt iffy at best. I was defeated and bereft. I didn't want to talk to God even though I knew that I needed Him. One day, three strangers knocked on the door of my apartment. It was late summer, the air muggy before a storm. I opened the door, despite my misgivings about strangers. I found three elderly folks from the church I was visiting who were out making sure the newcomers felt welcome in their church.

A surprising friendship developed with these three strangers. They invited me to attend their Sunday morning Bible study. I went because they were so kind to me. I was already leery of Christians by that point in my life, yet God used His people to touch my heart with His love. It was their love that drew me in. A few months later, they asked me to start teaching the Bible study class. I couldn't believe they would pick me to do something like that. Somehow, I said yes despite my insecurities. That was the year I fell in love with teaching the Bible. God's gift on my life to teach His word was awakened in the aftermath of my pain. I hadn't asked for it, but I've learned that God has a way of surprising us in our most painful places.

The next decade was dedicated to this calling—the teaching of God's Word. It took some time for me to get over the pain of rejection. I still wrestle with God over the details of my personal life, but when I consider the big movements of God in my ministry and calling, I can think of two big watershed moments. You've just heard the first. The second breakthrough came a few years later in the wake of leaving my church and the devastation I felt through it.

If I was skeptical of God's people before I left my church, after serving under corrupted leadership my faith in Christian leaders utterly shattered. I told myself I still loved Jesus and would survive this, but my skepticism about God and His church grew deeper. It was in the middle of my mess that, once again, God would redirect my calling. Here I was, a Bible teacher without a church body and a growing animosity toward organized Christianity. I felt dislocated from the very people I was called to serve. I wanted a fresh start—preferably in Tahiti. But God had other ideas.

Shortly after I left my church, a friend of mine who had, as it happens, left the same church a couple of years earlier invited me to go to Jordan with a team of Christians looking to do work with Syrian refugees. The year was 2013, and the Syrian refugee crisis was just beginning. I was just happy to be invited to get on a plane and head far from home.

That trip changed my life. I saw God at work globally and came to the obvious conclusion that if anyone could help Syrian refugees, it was me. I was Lebanese, spoke Arabic, and practiced medicine. It was a matter of months before we took our first medical missions trip to Lebanon to start our work with Syrian refugees there.

Once more, God had stepped in with His plans for my life, and I thank Him now that He did. My vision for my life used to be so limited. For months after leaving my church, I gave the people who hurt me so much power over my life. Yet they weren't the ones who had called me to ministry. God was. And they weren't the ones in control of my future. God was. I just couldn't see it clearly for a while. When our vision is disrupted by our pain, it is God's grace that restores our vision for who He is and what He longs to accomplish in us.

Today our work with Syrian refugees is alive and thriving. We still partner with ministries on the ground in Lebanon and continue to provide humanitarian aid in the form of food, housing, education, and medical care for thousands of people each month. I've been offered a front-row seat in an adventure I never could have dreamed up if not for God redirecting my calling at a time when I was facing the biggest rejection of my life.

Have you ever bought a box of strawberries and opened it up to find one rotten strawberry? Of course you have. We all have. When that happens, we don't throw away the entire box of strawberries. We assume that there was one bad fruit in the bunch and we go on eating the rest of the strawberries. When it comes to church hurt, too many people have found one or two bad strawberries in that box of strawberries and have decided to throw away not just the whole box but, in their pain, have made the resolve never to eat another strawberry again. It doesn't make sense.

I used to think that church hurt was a wound that would heal and leave a scar and that eventually everyone got better. Church hurt is more like a latent infection. Once you get it, it's always there. Like mono, it can go dormant for a long time, then just like that, stress will flare it up. With each flare comes the pain. The flares can be sporadic or recurrent, and each is accompanied with agonizing pain known only to those who suffer from that same pain.

I'm not sure where you are on the pain scale when it comes to wounds by other Christians. Maybe you're still scratching your head wondering, "Is this how Christians are supposed to act?" Typically, when you're asking that question, the answer is a resounding, "No, it's not!" Christians are supposed to love, not wound. But while we can't

control what other people do to us, we can control our responses to
the pain they inflict on us.

We've now come to the place in the book where we need some
real talk about forgiveness.

## Forgiveness

So many questions arise when we think about forgiveness:

Is forgiveness truly the only way to freedom?
Do the words matter or does the heart behind the words
matter too?
How do you truly forgive someone when you don't feel like
forgiving them at all?
What if the person who hurt you hasn't asked for forgiveness?
Is it truly forgiveness if it's not permanent?
What happens when you get a flare-up of anger over and over
again?

"Forgiveness" is a hard word to hear when I'm still feeling the
weight of the inflicted pain. Instead of forgiveness, I want to talk
about revenge and vindication. I gravitate toward Psalm 35 where the
psalmist takes comfort in God destroying his enemy. I don't prefer
Christian sermon clichés about letting go of my pain. Pain can be a
security blanket of sorts. It reminds me of the reality of my wounds.
Pain validates my wounds when no one else will. If you've ever had
a burn, then you know that deeper burns hurt more than superficial
ones. There are two places where the pain finally stops: either the
burn is so deep that it causes numbness to the nerve endings, or on
the other end of the spectrum, eventually healing takes place and the
pain resolves. The latter is what we're going after here.

But how? How do you truly forgive someone who has wounded

you when all you feel in your heart is disdain and even hatred toward that person? How do you come to terms with the fact that you call yourself a Christian but can't stand some of God's people?

Most Christian books tell us that it takes an act of your will to forgive someone. You've got to resolve to say the words before you feel them. I've tried that. The problem with that plan is that it can be skin deep. Words don't always change the heart.

Here's what I am learning about forgiveness:

There's a time to be angry, and a time to let go.
There's a time to lament, and a time to surrender that anger that's about to destroy you.
There's a time to say the words of forgiveness, and a time to feel them.
There's a time to talk about your wounds with others, and a time to stop.
There's a time to forgive, and a time to forgive again, and again.
And then there's a time to bow the knee before the Father in the darkness of night and confess that *there is a fate worse than living angry with God, and it's to live without God completely.*

A friend recently told me that forgiveness means releasing someone from the debt they owe you for the hurt they caused you. As much as I love magic pills, when it comes to forgiveness, there is no magic pill that ensures our feelings will change. Forgiveness is indeed an act of your will but not in the way I used to assume it was. When I was wounded by others, I felt like they owed me something. I wanted them to pay me back for the hurt they had caused me. But forgiveness asked that I let go of the debt others owed me because someone had already paid for it on their behalf.

I'm talking about Jesus now. He modeled this kind of forgiveness on the cross. He was guiltless, yet He was wronged. He deserved to be vindicated by His Father, but instead suffered in silence. He took the punishment that every one of us deserved so that we could stand in front of those who hurt us, certain that a price for sin had been paid. That price was paid by a God who loves justice so much that He was willing to die for the sake of justice.

Peter understood the power of what Jesus had done when he urged us to follow Christ's example. He wrote:

> For to this you have been called, because Christ also suffered for you, leaving you an example, so that you might follow in his steps. He committed no sin, neither was deceit found in his mouth. When he was reviled, he did not revile in return; when he suffered, he did not threaten, *but continued entrusting himself to him who judges justly.* (1 Peter 2:21–23)

We forget that last bit. Forgiveness doesn't just mean that a wounded person simply lets go of the offense. It means that we turn the offense over to God and allow Him to judge justly. In other words, healing when you've been wounded by other Christians has more to do with trusting God than you might have thought.

Instead of finding freedom in forgiveness, I wasted a few years supposedly protecting myself from other Christians. I stopped going to church for a season. My faith took a hit. I didn't trust God enough to pray like I used to. I had a decision to make: Would I hang on to my hurt, or would I choose to be free? The thing about God is that He's quite fair in what He asks of us.

God doesn't ask us to deny the pain that's been inflicted on us.
God doesn't ask us to minimize the pain we feel.
God doesn't ask us to bury our pain or ignore it.
God doesn't even ask us to understand our pain.

God simply asks us to turn over our pain to a loving Father
who is more than able to do the right thing on our behalf,
even when we least expect Him to and always when we
don't expect Him to anymore.

And there are also times when God uses our pain to move us out
of a horrible situation and to propel us into action.

### A Time to Leave

Sometimes, despite our best intentions, relationships do need boundaries. Sometimes they even need to end. Sometimes the next best step
is to move on: find another church, join another small group, look for
another job, move to another town if you must. It took me a while
to realize that even in the church, our happily ever after sometimes
won't come until later—when Jesus rules over the earth in the new
kingdom. As an idealist, it took me a while to accept that relationships will change. People grow and sometimes we drift apart. Though
reconciliation is at the heart of being a follower of Jesus, restitution
is not always a foregone conclusion. Trust is rebuilt over time but
eventually, most people can be trusted again. You will find a new
church and a new job and new friends and new relationships. You
might even find new love . . . though I'm still working on that one.

Even Paul understood the tension between staying and working things out versus walking away from a painful relationship. In
Romans 12, he wrote: "Bless those who persecute you; bless and do
not curse them (v. 14) . . . Live in harmony with one another (v. 16)
. . . Repay no one evil for evil, but give thought to do what is honor-
able in the sight of all" (v. 17). Then, almost as an after-thought but
important enough to make it into the canon of Scripture, he adds
in verse 18: "If possible, so far as it depends on you, live peaceably
with all."

If possible. As much as you can.

Sometimes, no matter how hard we try, it's best to leave. But leaving and forgiveness are not mutually exclusive. You can leave and still hang on to anger or you can leave and find the freedom that your soul needs. That freedom is found in forgiveness. Forgiveness is a matter of your heart. You can forgive someone even if you never get a chance to hear them tell you they're sorry. Forgiveness is about putting your whole weight in the goodness of God, who will never let it go. He made sure of that by allowing Jesus to take the brutal penalty of our pain on His body on a cross. Because He was wounded, we can be free.

## Your Wounds Are Your Teachers

I've done so many things wrong in my Christian life, but there are a couple of things I've gotten right. I've learned from my wounds. When my wounds became my teachers, my faith finally started to grow. While it was forgiveness that set me free, it was my wounds that allowed me to grow. It was through my wounds that I came to understand that God's grace in my failure awakens me to extend grace toward others in their failures too. It was through my wounds that I learned that the more I build my identity on who Christ says I am, the less I am concerned about what other people say about me. It was my wounds that gave me empathy for other people's pain. *I've learned that what I see as massive failure in my life, God sees as a massive opportunity to redirect my calling.*

Our willingness to let go of our pain unlocks God's purposes in our lives. Forgiveness is the key to

> I've learned that what I see as massive failure in my life, God sees as a massive opportunity to redirect my calling.

87

stepping into our calling. Thankfully, God propels us out of our pain even before we reach the place where we've learned to forgive well. The Christian life is a process, a process that hinges on God. Most of us don't have enough grace for ourselves to make it, but thankfully, it's God's grace toward us that we need the most: God doing on our behalf what we cannot accomplish on our own, including forgiveness of those who have hurt us.

So how do you find your way back to God when you've been wounded by other Christians? You do what only you can do, and you let God do what only He can do. You choose to forgive and you let God do the vindication.

## The Aftermath

My day of vindication did eventually come. In time, the church I had left blew up at the leadership level. The pastor was disqualified from ministry by the elders. In that moment, I did feel seen by God. I felt loved and affirmed. I felt Romans 8:28 deep in my bones, that all things do work together for good for those who love God. I don't take joy in the way my story played out because there were many wounded in the aftermath, many who are still recovering from their own wounds. Few things have hurt the cause of Christianity more than the pain inflicted on Christians by other Christians. But when justice comes, there is an unexplainable joy in knowing that God is faithful.

Your story is not over yet. If you're still stuck in a painful situation, I know this chapter is a heavy one. You might be wrestling with whether to stay and try to work things out with the person who has hurt you or you might be coming to terms with the reality that it's high time you leave. I might not have specific answers for your situation, but what I can promise you is that you're not alone. You're not unseen. God has not forgotten you. Take a deep breath. Fix your eyes on Jesus. He is just, and He is good. Then reach out to someone who will believe you and who will help you. Use them. Get help. And believe that your story is not over. You will live past this chapter of your life.

If you're reeling from past wounds inflicted by other Christians, rest assured that this book is not just about me—it's about you too. It's about your life and your future. It's a book about how God is using your suffering to guide you to your purpose. This is the story of how God is redirecting your calling through your failures and wounds and feelings of rejection. Trust Him enough to write the rest of your story. Trust Him enough to vindicate you someday. Trust Him enough to heal you completely.

It's time to let go of your hurt.

**SPEND A FEW MINUTES CONSIDERING THESE QUESTIONS, and bring your thoughts and feelings to God in prayer:**

*Think of someone you'd like to forgive. How can you forgive him or her when you don't feel like doing so?*

*Is it truly forgiveness if it's not permanent or you experience flare-ups of anger?*

*What can we remember about forgiveness, given the example of Christ?*

*Chapter 5*

# IS GOD REALLY FAIR?

No matter how you look at it, God isn't really fair, at least not in the way we, as human beings, define "fair."

I mean, you're two pages into reading the Bible when you find out that God destroyed the entire world in a flood. Only eight people survived—a man named Noah and his family. Just six chapters into the creation of a beautiful world and God ends it all because humankind was basically evil. Only Noah was saved because he *believed* God.

People have a problem with the Old Testament. If I'm being honest, it's not hard to understand why. The Old Testament is full of stories of death and violence and rape and injustice. In the case of Sodom and Gomorrah, an entire village is destroyed for its sin of unbelief (Jude 5).

God's own chosen people, the people of Israel, are depicted again and again in a horrible light. Take for example Genesis 34. We read about Jacob's sons who got angry at a man named Shechem for sleeping with their sister Dinah and decided to kill him, even though he wanted to set things right by marrying Dinah. Worse than their reaction is their execution of the murder. They set Shechem and his family up by suggesting they get circumcised as a display of loyalty to them, then killed the entire clan while they were recovering from the painful procedure. It's definitely not a story for Sunday school classroom flannelgraphs!

The Passover story, arguably the hinge story of the whole biblical narrative, ends up victorious for the people of Israel, but bloody for everyone else. The cost of the Passover was the death of every firstborn baby in the Egyptian kingdom.

The violence continues past the Exodus account. For forty years the people of Israel wandered in the wilderness toward the promised land. In those years they learned to fight. They learned to kill. They experienced death among their own. Exodus 32 is brutal. The people of Israel became impatient with God and erected an idol to worship. Later that day over 32,000 people died in a plague. These were God's own people who died!

The Bible can be a difficult book to read.

From a marketing perspective, some of its stories actually make God look bad to human consumers. They make God look unfair. Remember Uzzah in 2 Samuel 6:1–7? The poor guy was worshiping God around the ark of the covenant. When the ark threatened to fall, Uzzah, in an attempt to keep it from falling, reached out and touched the ark. God killed him for desecrating what was holy. *What? Can't God handle a human mistake?*

Many people today reject the Bible because it's easier to reject what we cannot understand than to dig deeper into understanding God. If nothing else, it seems safer to ignore the Bible than to submit to its teachings.

All that to say, if you've ever struggled with the God of the Bible, you're not alone.

Today only two out of ten Americans under age thirty believe attending church is important, and 59 percent of millennials raised in church have dropped out.[1] One of the main critiques millennials and others have against God is related to His perceived wrath. Why does God seem so angry all the time? Is it just the Old Testament that depicts an angry God? Today's Christians seem determined to distance themselves from the God of the Old Testament, choosing rather to hang on to the New Testament version of a God who always reveals Himself as love and grace.

Many who claim to be Christians long to redefine who God is based on their own understanding of what's fair. Perhaps the problem is that what seems fair to us in any particular situation isn't the same as what's just. And justice, when you think about it, isn't always fair. Whereas justice rests on what's right and moral and true, fairness boils down to my moral evaluation of what happened. When I speak of fairness, I speak of evenness. Justice is more. When God speaks of justice, He speaks truth.

## A Case of Deconstruction

In an act of providential timing, as I begin writing this chapter, I came across a story about a famous Christian who recently disclosed that he is leaving the Christian faith. He's the son of a pastor and the (former) lead singer of a popular Christian band.

"After growing up in a Christian home," he wrote on his Instagram page, "being a pastor's kid, playing and singing in a Christian band, and having the word 'Christian' in front of most of the things in my life—I am now finding that I no longer believe in God."[2]

Here's how he reached his conclusion:

"There were still many things about Christian culture that made me uncomfortable. . . . There were things that didn't make sense to me. If God is all loving, and all powerful, why is there evil in the world? Can he not do anything about it? Does he choose not to? Is the evil in the world a result of his desire to gives us free will? Okay then, what about famine and disease and floods and all the suffering that isn't caused by humans and our free will? If God is loving, why does he send people to hell?"

His crisis of faith is not novel; people have struggled with the problem of evil for centuries.

"My whole life people always said, 'You have to go back to what the Bible says,'" he wrote. "I found, however, that consulting and discussing the Bible didn't answer my questions, it only amplified them. Why does God seem so [angry] in most of the Old Testament, and then all of a sudden he's a loving father in the New Testament? Why does he say not to kill, but then instruct Israel to turn around and kill men women and children to take the promised land? Why does God let Job suffer horrible things just to . . . win a bet with Satan?! Why does he tell Abraham to kill his son (more killing again) then basically say just kidding! That was a test. Why does Jesus have to die for our sins (more killing again)? If God can do anything, can't he forgive without someone dying?"

He uncovers what he believes are inconsistencies in Scripture. His question soon shifts to doubt which sets up the deconstruction of his faith and the eventual disbelief in God he now publicly proclaims. He concludes:

"Once I found that I didn't believe the Bible was the perfect word of God—it didn't take long to realize that I was no longer sure he was there at all."[3]

Is God oblivious to how His Word makes Him look? Was it an act of divine error that allowed certain stories to make it into the canon of Scripture that are best kept with the dirty laundry? And if God intentionally includes the accounts of violence in His Word, who is this God and what are we to do with Him? Is He to be trusted? Is His Word to be trusted?

Two things are clear: these are questions worth asking, and the God of the Bible is *not* fair by human standards. The more we consider who God is and how He works, the more our concept of justice needs to be redefined.

## God Is Not Fair

Consider David, arguably the greatest king of Israel. He had an affair with a married woman named Bathsheba. If you grew up in the church you might have accepted the assumption that she gave her consent but, in a #metoo culture, it's hard to downplay the power dynamic between the King of Israel and Bathsheba. David got Bathsheba pregnant, then got her husband killed in battle in order to hide his sin. God knew the details and still allowed Bathsheba's husband Uriah the Hittite to die. For a while, it seemed as if David got away with murder. Eventually David was confronted with his sin. He repented, and there were consequences to his sinful choices, but today he's still known as a man after God's own heart.

The New Testament may not be as full of violence as the Old Testament, but God continues to hone in on this concept of what He deems to be fair.

My least favorite parable is the one that Jesus tells in Matthew 20:1–16. A man hires a worker early in the morning and agrees to pay him a denarius. At nine in the morning, he finds another worker and promises the same denarius for a day's work. At noon another laborer is hired for the same amount, and at 3 p.m. and at 5 p.m., a few more laborers are gathered, all promised that same measly denarius. Come payday, the landowner gathers the workers and pays them what was promised, a denarius each. Understandably, if you were hired at 5 p.m., payday sounds like a dream. But if you were hired early in the morning, it feels like a kick in the gut.

That's the story Jesus uses to illustrate life in the Kingdom. Which leads to the obvious questions: *Why? Why does Jesus highlight a parable that makes God look so unfair?*

Over and over again God seems to give mercy to those who deserve judgment. He punishes those who don't seem to deserve it. He longs to save the people we long to avoid, people like prostitutes and thieves and adulterers. While His ways sound noble at first, imagine a savior who gravitates towards the Bernie Madoffs and Harvey Weinsteins of our world. Doesn't seem so palatable, does it?

My first medical missions trip to the Middle East to serve Syrian refugees was eye-opening. Though I had grown up in Beirut and had lived through the horrific Lebanese civil war, I wasn't prepared for the stories I heard from the patients who, one after the other, walked through our clinic each day. Every mother had lost a child. Every child had lost their innocence in one way or another. Every family had lost material belongings. No one was protected from the atrocities of war.

As the refugees settled into their temporary tents in Lebanon, I learned more about the inequities in the world. Illiteracy was rampant among refugees. School was a luxury. Jobs were menial. Please understand that I'm not naïve to the pain in the world. I've spent the last two decades caring for the poor and marginalized in the ER. I've traveled to resource-poor countries repeatedly to provide people with medical care. But I wasn't prepared for the masses of people who were suffering just a stone's throw from my home country. Millions of people had become victims of evil simply because of where they were born. Their families of origin and their DNA put them in a place where basic survival was not guaranteed.

Where was God in *their* story?

Where was God in 1948 when my mother, a seven-year-old Palestinian kid, was kicked out of her home in Jerusalem along with her mother, father, and two siblings by the Israeli army with nothing but the shirts on their backs? Where was God when they landed in Lebanon months later, strangers in a land not their own, embarking on a new life where they would always be considered less than, unwanted, and undesirable?

Life is not fair. Most of us figured that out in elementary school.

Yet most of us still dream of a God who will set every wrong right someday. We dream of justice while we talk about what's fair.

### The Story of a Prophet Who Didn't Get It

There once was a prophet named Jonah. He didn't think God was fair either. One day, God asked Jonah to go to Nineveh and tell the people of Nineveh about God's love. Jonah freaked out. Did God have a clue what He was asking? The people of Nineveh were evil. They didn't deserve God. They were like today's ISIS fighters. They deserved to die for their sin. They had brutally hurt Jonah's people over the years. How dare God extend His love to them?

So Jonah refused. He said no to God and ran the other way. He figured he'd go to Tarshish. Tarshish was 180 degrees away, both physically and psychologically, from Nineveh. It was the place where people who wanted success and comfort went. Jonah was happy serving God in Tarshish with people who *deserved* love and mercy.

You may be familiar with the rest of the story. Jonah didn't get very far, because you see, God isn't fair. He cares about the hated, He fights for those who don't deserve it. He looks for the hurting and the lost, and He does it in ways we cannot comprehend.

It was a good thing for Jonah that God wasn't fair. Instead of punishing Jonah for disobeying Him, God gave Jonah a second chance in the form of a detour into the belly of a fish. And there, in the middle of isolation and darkness, Jonah learned about mercy—God's mercy.

*It's always easier to see God's mercy when we desperately need it. It's easier to see God as Savior when we need to be saved.*

Three days later, Jonah made it to Nineveh. It wasn't long after he started preaching about this mysteriously unfair God that revival broke out in Nineveh. You'd think the prophet would be glad. He wasn't. Jonah was devastated. How could God be so unfair? Why would a good God save such a bad people? What kind of God acts this way? My favorite part of this short book comes at the very end. Feeling sorry for himself, Jonah sits under a broom tree mourning his life. Once again, God reveals Himself to Jonah:

> "Do you do well to be angry for the plant? . . . You pity the plant, for which you did not labor, nor did you make it grow, which came into being in a night and perished in a night. And should not I pity Nineveh, that great city, in which there are more than 120,000 persons who do not know their right hand from their left, and also much cattle?" (Jonah 4:9–11)

The end. The story of Jonah ends without closure. Loose ends stay loose. Did Jonah's faith reconstruct? It's believed that Jonah wrote the little book that carries his name. Maybe Jonah did finally come to terms with the God of the Bible: a God of *both* mercy and justice, a God we cannot put in a box. We'll never know on this side of eternity!

### Break the Cycle of Hate

God is not always fair and it's one of the best things to know about the God of the Bible. Oh, He's just, but that justice is fair depending on your perspective.

Ask the people of Syria who fled from their homeland and sought protection in Lebanon. If you know much about Middle Eastern politics, then you might know that Lebanon and Syria are two countries with lots of baggage and a complicated history between them. When the Syrian refugees arrived in Lebanon, they expected rejection by the Lebanese people, and they got it. But they found welcome in the Lebanese church among Christians.

The pastor I work with in Lebanon tells his side of the story.

When the Syrians showed up at his church seeking food and humanitarian aid, the pastor had to decide: Do I do what's fair and hate the Syrians as every good Lebanese should do? Or do I treat them like Jesus would, not because they deserve it, but because they need it? One day, while the pastor was reading his Bible and wrestling with God over the matter, he became overwhelmed by God's undeserved love for him and decided to break the cycle of hate. He chose to feed his enemy.

After decades of war and political tension between the Lebanese and the Syrians, *to hate the Syrians was his right, but to love them was his privilege.* Many in his church did not think he should get involved with helping the Syrians. But Christians don't follow a fair God. He does what we cannot comprehend; He loves the unlovable. He calls us to do the same.

Today his church serves thousands of Syrian refugees. The church has seen thousands of Syrian refugees give their lives to Jesus. God's deep, deep love turned everything upside down for that pastor. But that love had a cost. The cost was God Himself. God became human in the form of Jesus and died on the cross to pay the price for sin. This might sound like Sunday school jargon to your ears, but it's God's honest truth.

### The Greatest Injustice of All

Four hundred years after the Old Testament was written, God's chosen people, the people of Israel, were a mess. God had predicted their condition and warned them about what was to come. But they couldn't help themselves. They didn't believe God. They had chosen their own ways. And for four hundred years, they endured God's silence. If there's one thing worse than God's anger, it's His silence. And for four hundred years, God said nothing, or at least nothing that was recorded in the canon of Scripture.

Imagine the pain of that silence. Or maybe you don't have to.

Do you ever wonder why the God of the Old Testament seems so much more violent than the God of the New Testament? On that day on the cross, all of God's wrath focused on Jesus. In that moment on the cross, Jesus bore the wrath of God on our behalf. In His last breath, Jesus pleaded for forgiveness for others: "Father, forgive them, for they know not what they do" (Luke 23:34).

Then He died.

On the tragic night of Passover, as told in the Old Testament, when every firstborn in Egypt was killed, the people of Israel were safe not because they were good. They were safe because of the blood of the lamb. God had instructed the people of Israel to kill a lamb, an unblemished lamb, and to put its blood on the doorpost. Every home covered by the blood lived. Those who did not have the blood covering lost their firstborn.

The God of the Old Testament is the same God of the New Testament. He's a God of love *and* of justice. He's a God who is not fair. He's a God who grants forgiveness and freedom to everyone who puts their trust in Him—not because we deserve it but because a price has been paid for our sin.

Jesus lived. He died. And He rose again. No one could have made His story up. His tomb is still empty. His disciples who hid in fear on the day of His crucifixion would eventually give their lives for His sake. Their lives were turned upside down, not just because they spent three years hanging out with a man named Jesus, but because they had been radically transformed by the resurrected Savior—a Savior who had paid the price for their sins.

Could God have saved the world without blood and the death of Jesus? The former Christian band singer proposes that forgiveness be just that: "My parents taught me to forgive people— nobody dies in that scenario."[4] Easy-peasy, but unfounded.

The reason nobody dies in that scenario is because someone did die once. Justice demanded that a price be paid for wrongdoing. God in His holiness cannot overlook sin. Sin's cost is death. The day that Adam and Eve fell in the garden, sin entered the world and the need for a Savior was born. All the way back in Genesis 3, God promises the coming of a Savior from the seed of the woman. The entire story of the Bible becomes the story of redemption. The biblical narrative works its way all the way up to the life of Jesus, the perfect lamb of God. Noah found shelter in the ark, which is symbolic of us finding shelter in Jesus today. Abraham didn't have to kill his son because a substitute was found in the form of a ram. The people of Israel were spared at Passover because the blood of a spotless lamb had been painted on the posts of their doors. The entire Old Testament builds up to its climax: the birth of the promised Messiah in the form of the Son of Man, named Jesus.

Emmanuel means "God with us." At the onset of the New Testament, we see God taking the form of a man born to a humble woman named Mary, a virgin who conceived through the Holy Spirit. Jesus grows up as a carpenter, lives a perfect life, and at the age of thirty, His ministry begins. For three years He proves He is God through miracles and teachings and key encounters with people. He ministers just three years before He is arrested and crucified. The crucifixion did not come as a surprise to Jesus. He spent His entire earthly ministry predicting His death and assuring His followers that He came to die. They didn't understand Him in the way many don't understand the need for His death today. He was crucified on the cross and three days later, He rose from the dead as He had predicted He would.

Is this the most bizarre story you've ever heard? Is Christ's death the most unfair story you'll ever hear? It's unfair in the magnitude of God's love toward us and our lukewarm acceptance of Him most of the time. It's unfair in that it allows us to gain where Christ received nothing but our pain. Yet God has never been about fairness. And because God is unfair, our perfect God becomes sin for us so that we could be made free.

The unfair news of the gospel is that in Jesus Christ justice is fully served and mercy is fully received. It's the best news in the world, and a true picture of grace. Jesus shed His blood in the most violent act in human history to bear the wrath of God for the forgiveness of our sin. God lovingly accepted Christ's death as payment for our sin. All we have to do is accept it.

> **The most "unfair" thing God ever did was offer His gift of salvation to anyone who would receive it.**

So whether you're an ISIS fighter or Mother Teresa, *the most "unfair" thing God ever did was offer His gift of salvation to anyone who would receive it.* It doesn't matter if you're hired early in the morning or at five in the afternoon. You're given grace because of the simple fact that God is not fair, but a loving, just God.

## Good News for People Like Us

My friend Rod is a pastor in Grand Rapids, Michigan, a predominantly white area. He is trying to teach his congregation about racial reconciliation. Ask most black people in the United States, and they'll tell you: life isn't fair. Ask most black Christians in American churches and they'll tell you: the church isn't fair. Rod recently told his people, "If you are angry about God's anger and justice, then you might just be a people of privilege. If you are a victim, you are *counting* on God's anger and justice." Rod understood that for many victims, it is the hope of God's future justice that keeps them hanging on for a better tomorrow. *Justice ensures that fairness is served. Mercy ensures that fairness is not. God is both in the person of Christ.*

Job struggled to understand God in the midst of his pain. He didn't feel God was fair. He felt like God had given him worse than he deserved. God didn't deliver him in the speed that he had hoped for. Job spent a long time lamenting and asking questions about his life.

He said a lot in the first thirty-eight chapters of Job. In those first chapters, we witness a man struggling to make sense of his life and his God. Job's faith was *almost* deconstructed until God finally spoke up:

"Who is this that darkens counsel by words without knowledge? Dress for action like a man; I will question you, and you make it known to me," God said to Job in Job 38:2–3.

That's when Job finally stopped talking. Job learned that it's impossible to keep on talking once we start clearly hearing the voice of the Lord.

> **Justice ensures that fairness is served. Mercy ensures that fairness is not. God is both in the person of Christ.**

C. S. Lewis wrote a profound essay titled *God in the Dock* (in the British court system, the accused stands in the dock; we might change the title to "God on Trial" instead). According to Lewis,

the ancient man approached God (or even the gods) as the accused person approaches his judge. For the modern man the roles are reversed. He is the judge: God is in the dock. He is quite a kindly judge: if God should have a reasonable defence for being the god who permits war, poverty and disease, he is ready to listen to it. The trial may even end in God's acquittal. But the important thing is that Man is on the Bench and God in the Dock.[5]

When it comes to justice and what's fair, we all think we're the experts. We declare "I believe in God" or its opposite "I don't believe in God." We assume the right to choose whether or not we approve of His ways and believe in Him or not. We think we know what's right and how the world should run.

It doesn't work this way.

He is the creator. We are the created.

He is the potter. We are the clay.

## Making It Personal

Do you struggle with God's justice? Has your struggle led you away from believing God?

Do you struggle to trust a God who's watching millions of people die of hunger and diseases, a God who allows child abusers and sex traffickers to go free in this lifetime and doesn't protect the unborn? Do you struggle to believe that God is just when your husband has gotten away with humiliating you while everyone assumes he's the model elder in your church? Do you struggle with God's fairness when you've been mistreated by your church leaders and you've been excommunicated by the church while those evil leaders continue to grow their kingdoms in the name of Jesus?

On the night of the crucifixion, everyone assumed that Jesus had lost. Everyone assumed that His time was up, that justice was thwarted, that God had forgotten to show up.

On the morning of the resurrection everyone found out that they were wrong.

God *did* show up. God *had* seen. God had not forgotten. God *knew*.

Is God fair? Thank God He is not.

Is God good? In your darkest seasons, read the psalms and rest assured that He is.

Is God angry? Not anymore. His anger has been absorbed by Jesus forevermore.

And because of Jesus, life will never be fair again.

You don't have to defend the Bible. You don't have to prove to every skeptic that God is just and good at the same time. You don't even have to agree with His ways. You don't have to worry about how others perceive this God who gave His life for you. All God asks is that you trust Him. The same God who saved Noah, the same God who called Abraham, the same God who restored Job, and the same God who lovingly used Jonah, is the same God who is waiting for you with open arms, urging you closer to His heart, even when you can't fully understand His ways.

So yes, you can trust God's goodness, even when His ways aren't always what we think of as fair.

**SPEND A FEW MINUTES WITH THESE QUESTIONS,
and bring your thoughts and feelings to God in prayer:**

*What's the difference between justice and fairness?*

*Have you ever felt that God is unfair?*

*Where do you see God in the world's suffering?*

*Chapter 6*

# IS *THIS* THE NORMAL CHRISTIAN LIFE?

It was a classic tale of two brothers.

From the very start, God had a plan. Two boys were conceived in one womb. Their mother, a praying woman, felt the tension early in her pregnancy. When she looked to God for the reason behind the struggle, He told her about the kids' destinies. The younger would lead, and the older would serve the younger. The whole predicament countered cultural expectations, but God had spoken, and it would surely come to pass.

The boys were named Esau and Jacob. It took just a few years into their adolescence for the prophecy to be fulfilled. Esau chose his appetite over his birthright, and the rest, as they say, was history, but a complicated history at that. Even though Jacob was the chosen one, he was a deceiving scoundrel who grabbed every opportunity he could find to ensure that his destiny was secure.

The entire family saga came to a head one day when Isaac, the father of the twins, was on his deathbed. He called his favored son Esau, his firstborn, and asked him to prepare him a meal before receiving his blessing. The boys' mother Rebekah overheard the conversation and told Jacob, her favorite son, about it. If you have a mother, then you know no one can pull a quick one over on Mama Bear, and sure enough, Rebekah helped Jacob deceive his father into thinking he was Esau and set him up to receive the blessing.

When Esau found out, he was furious. He decided to kill Jacob. Jacob believed the threat and under the counsel of both his parents, decided to run for his life. Talk about a dysfunctional family! For a guy who had already been chosen by God to carry on the family blessing and legacy, Jacob's life didn't look so great at that point.

On the night he fled home, Jacob camped out under the stars using a rock for a pillow. He was alone and afraid. That night, Jacob had a dream. Meanwhile, Esau settled down a little but not before marrying a Canaanite in an act of direct rebellion against God and his parents and upbringing.

One messed-up God-fearing home, two messed-up young men; one leaves home to live in rebellion to his upbringing, the other leaves alone and confused, uncertain of who God is, uncertain of the future.

Sounds a lot like many modern-day Christian families.

We live in what can only be called a "post-Christian" time. Many sociologists and church historians and leaders have wondered why our young people are dropping out of church life. Some days, panic about the future of the church sets in; other days, optimism is touted in an effort to encourage the churchgoing masses.

In reality, it is nothing more than a tale of two brothers. We have watched an entire generation of kids grow up in Christian homes. They heard the gospel at a young age. They've been introduced to God through their parents. They are now old enough to make their own choices: Will they let their disappointments in life derail them or reshape them? Will they return to the faith of their childhoods? Will they find their way back to church again?

Esau rejected his parents' faith, while Jacob had a lot of growing up still to do.

It's not always easy to discern which kids in the youth group have embraced true faith in Jesus Christ. *A Christianity born out of duty* and tradition will never sustain you through life's trials, while a Christianity rooted in a love relationship with Jesus will carry you through anything. While the crisis of young people leaving the church is real, the crisis we need is the crisis of faith that will differentiate true faith vs. inauthentic faith.

> **What we often call a crisis of faith is simply the normal Christian life.**

In other words, it's not a matter of *if* but *when* you'll have a crisis of faith. There is a crisis of faith that is endured that turns out to be an essential part of the discipleship process. It's part of making your faith your own. It's part of your maturing process in Christ. *What we often call a crisis of faith is simply the normal Christian life.*

### Redefining Disillusionment

A few months before I started writing this book, I was having my own faith crisis. It wasn't my first and will likely not be my last. This particular crisis was rooted in some of my ministry expectations. I decided to get some help in the form of an operations and strategy expert named Doug.

The first four hours of our meeting were spent creating a map of my life. We started in grade school and made our way to present-day events, dividing my life into "crises" or "landmarks." The latter included things like my medical school graduation and writing my first book. The former list was a list of my failures, both personal and professional. After using a white board to sketch out a linear distribution of the events in my life, Doug had me divide my life into three big time periods and then asked me to name each stage of my life.

The first stage was easy to name: new life in Christ. This stage was all about new beginnings and the excitement of starting a journey with God. It was about feeling chosen and loved by God. It was about victories and open doors and dreaming big for God. It was about getting into medical school and graduating and making it into my first-choice residency. It was a season of good news and favor. (I liked stage 1 a lot!)

Stage 2 was more challenging. I felt a lump in my throat when I looked at my life in stage 2 spread over a period of fifteen years. My first heartbreak. A broken engagement. A deep aching loneliness. Stage 2 was the stage where God called me into ministry, followed by the unexpected strain of His moving me into a new town where I knew no one. These were the days I started blogging in an effort to just do something for God. I struggled to find a church in stage 2 but eventually landed in my dream church where my hope to be in ministry was renewed. Stage 2 was also the time when I walked through my church pain. A second broken engagement. While stage 2 was where I wrote my first book, then my second and my third, it was also in this stage that I faced my inability to accomplish my God-given dreams in my own strength. I felt like a failure despite what others called a success.

I could only see one thing as I stared at stage 2, so I spoke it out loud: *disillusionment.*

Doug's eyebrow lifted a touch, "Disillusionment? That's what you see here?" I was smart enough not to answer. "Try again," he offered. My blank look was a clue for Doug to step in with the answer: "I see your calling in stage 2. What you see as disillusionment, I see as the normal Christian life."

I was dumbfounded—so much so that I don't think we ever quite made it to stage 3.

I had never thought of my life that way, but there it was, laid bare before my very eyes. The very things that had almost derailed me from my faith and calling were the very things God had used, not just to redirect me but to deepen my love and dependence on Him.

The very things that I had hated were the very tools God had used to grow me into the person that I was.

I have come to see that Doug was right: what we call "disillusionment" in our faith is often just the normal Christian life. Perhaps it's time we hear this more regularly in the church. Too many of today's youth groups are focused on entertaining its young, with some doctrine thrown in for good measure, but not enough to turn the masses away. Young people lean into messages that promise God's favor in their lives. They underline verses that promise good things in their lives and judge God's goodness by the number of likes they get on social media posts. By the time churches send their young folks into life after high school, they have taught them how to play the part of a popular Christian speaker or worship leader but have by and large missed the opportunity to disciple them. Their maturity is an inch deep and will not sustain the assault on their faith that's sure to come in this broken world.

Is the church to blame for the weak discipleship produced in today's well-lit, multi-site churches? Are parents to blame for the shaky faith of their sons and daughters? Is our culture to blame for the ungodly influences luring young Christians into disbelief? Are celebrity pastors to blame for wrongly modeling what it means to be a true follower of Jesus? Is the big evangelical complex to blame for monetizing Christianity?

Perhaps nobody is to blame. Instead of playing the blame game, what young people need to be lovingly and clearly taught is that when they leave home and experience a crisis of faith, they are simply living the normal Christian life. It can be painful, but if they know it's coming, they might be able to navigate it more smoothly.

On the night that Jacob ran away from home to escape the ire of his twin brother Esau, he was alone and afraid. He fell asleep that night and had a dream. In his dream, God dropped a ladder from heaven with angels going up and down the ladder. In his dream, God made Jacob a promise:

> "I am the LORD, the God of Abraham your father and the God of Isaac. The land on which you lie I will give to you and to your offspring. Your offspring shall be like the dust of the earth, and you shall spread abroad to the west and to the east and to the north and to the south, and in you and your offspring shall all the families of the earth be blessed. Behold, I am with you and will keep you wherever you go, and will bring you back to this land. For I will not leave you until I have done what I have promised you." (Gen. 28:13–15)

**A disciple is one who has counted the cost of following Christ and found Him to be their greatest treasure.**

This was the first real crisis in Jacob's life, but not the last. This crisis was about Jacob's faith becoming his own. Though God had already made the same promise to Jacob's father and grandfather, the time had come for Jacob himself to embrace the Lord. It was time for Jacob to experience God through His Word and to learn about Him through His works. Jacob's adventure with God was about to begin.

### Real Discipleship

Perhaps you are much older and wiser than Jacob but find yourself struggling with your faith. I am learning that we don't wrestle with God just once in our lives. We wrestle with Him over and over again, and each time leads us into a deeper knowledge of who He is and a deeper dependence on Him.

Discipleship is all about experiencing God through His Word and through His works. A disciple is one who has counted the cost of following Christ and found Him to be their greatest treasure. Discipleship is about experiencing Christ as the supreme pleasure. This kind of discipleship will never happen without a struggle. This kind of Christianity is too important not to demand a fight. We struggle because of our own flesh that still hasn't gotten the memo that it's now dead. We struggle because of Satan, who hates everything about Jesus and His children. We struggle because of the broken world we live in with all of its pain and trials. To struggle is the normal life, but to struggle victoriously should be the normal Christian life for every growing disciple of Jesus.

In order to become a mature follower of Jesus, every Christian will have to experience this process of growth. For Jacob, that night where he had the ladder dream was the beginning of his journey. The next twenty years were hard for Jacob. He endured much pain and recurrent disappointment. He encountered challenges in his love life. He encountered challenges with his in-laws. By the time Jacob left Haran, he was a changed man. Despite the fact that God had chosen Jacob to secure Abraham's lineage and legacy, God did not spare Jacob the pain of life. In fact, it was this very suffering in the life of Jacob that would be the pathway to his purpose. It was his very longings that would draw him closer to the heart of God in expectation. It was his failures that redirected his life to his calling, and it was God's justice that would eventually lead Jacob back home. That's when Jacob got his second lesson in surrender.

Have you ever felt stuck in an emotional wilderness?

Have you ever felt God calling you to do something only to find trouble at every corner?

Have you ever felt so overwhelmed by your faltering faith that you lost sight of God's presence in your life?

That's where Jacob found himself after leaving Haran to go back home.

## Wrestling with God

In Genesis 32, Jacob is alone and he's afraid. God was the one who told Jacob to head back home, but God had not given him the heads-up that Esau was headed his way. Even after twenty years away, Jacob is still petrified of his brother. He's in the familiar wilderness again, in the middle of a sleepless night, but this time, instead of a dream, Jacob has a wrestling match with God.

Have you ever wrestled with God? Have you ever struggled through the night with God, wondering why your life has turned out like it has, overwhelmed by your future? We wrestle with God in an attempt to convince Him to do what we want. We fight with God until we're worn out and then, just like Jacob, we hang on by a thread. *It is only when we've got nothing left to fight with that we let go and realize that God's still got His hold on us.* I call that "letting go" surrender, and it's the safest place to live as a follower of Jesus.

"What's your name?" God asks Jacob.

Jacob answers as honestly as he could: "Jacob," meaning "deceiver." The meaning is not lost on God. Jacob is indeed a deceiver. Years later and Jacob still can't shake the shame of all the ways that he's lied and deceived. He still sees himself as his worst self. Despite decades with God, he still believes he is his broken identity. Yet even in Jacob's darkest hour, God provides unyielding grace: "Your name shall no longer be called Jacob, but Israel, for you have striven with God and with men, and have prevailed" (Gen. 32:28).

God always sees the best version of who we are. He sees past our shame to all the places He still wants to take us. He sees our end from the beginning and our current spot from the end. God knows that it's only when we come to the end of ourselves that we will finally see His face. Grace calls us by our real names, sees our God-given identities, and opens our eyes to see God's presence and goodness in our despair.

That's what growing up is. Spiritual maturity is about accepting our God-given identities. It's about understanding who we are without Christ and receiving by grace who God makes us in Christ. Christian maturity is our ability to see God's hand in our most difficult circumstance and in our confusion. It's about trusting God with the outcome in our lives. Christian maturity is about escaping the exhaustion of trying to control the outcomes by releasing whatever it is that's holding us back.

Jacob spent twenty years in Haran in what looks like an utter waste in the life of Jacob, yet those years were the making of Jacob. *This* is the normal Christian life—it is the life God chooses for us with all of its trials and landmarks and all of its highs and lows. It is the life God uses to make us who He longs for us to be in Christ, and it will only happen when we let go and rest in Him alone.

## Your Faith Crisis

Every faith crisis is meant to reveal the truth about who you are. If you've never embraced true faith, all it will take is a small crisis to cause you to wander away from the faith. You can't lose what you never had. It's what happened to Esau. He valued the wrong things. He was driven by his appetites. He never understood God's heart for him. He consistently chose what felt good now and sacrificed what is good forever. He was brought up in the same home as Jacob, with the same parents, and given the same education and values, but Esau never had true faith. When the storm hit, Esau's false faith floundered.

Jacob, on the other hand, simply needed to grow up. Jacob needed to experience God for himself. And Jacob, like his grandfather

Abraham before him, learned to build altars to God in each crisis of faith he lived through.

Jacob learned to say yes to God over and over and over again. That's what discipleship is—saying yes to God over and over and over again. To say yes to God, we're saying yes to transformation. To say yes to God is an invitation to grow. To say yes is an invitation to sometimes misunderstand what God is doing, but to always trust His goodness even when we're hurting. To say yes to God is to put all of our eggs in His basket. It will sometimes take a wrestling match with God to finally say yes to Him. Wrestling doesn't show a weak faith. It is the exercise that helps strengthen it.

This is the normal Christian life. Few are told what the normal Christian life will look like. Few are warned of the difficulties that lie ahead. Few are prepared for the road, and few truly believe that God remains constant and good even when it hurts. Does discipleship have to hurt? The answer is yes, it does. The normal Christian life hurts because it always involves death: the death of self, the death of my will, the death of my pride, my names, and my identity. But it was Jesus who taught us that "unless a grain of wheat falls into the earth and dies, it remains alone; but if it dies, it bears much fruit" (John 12:24). It was Jesus who said, "If anyone would come after me, let him deny himself and take up his cross daily and follow me" (Luke 9:23).

Did you think this kind of death would be easy? Did you think surrender would be easy? Think again.

After his wrestling match with God, Jacob limped. His faith crisis did not leave him unchanged, and everyone could see it. A limp is a sign of dependence. You can't go as fast or as far with a limp. You need the help of others when you walk with a limp. That limp would be a reminder to Jacob for the rest of his life of his utter need for the Lord. The best fruit that will ever come out of a crisis of faith is found in our limps. It's the fruit of brokenness. Your limp is a reminder that you can't do it alone. The normal Christian life is a life of growing dependence on the Lord.

Do you long for your crisis of faith to end?

Are you ready for the reconstruction of your faith?

Your struggle won't end until you're willing to be broken. The only way your faith can be reconstructed is in this place of surrender. The moment you agree with God about who you are, things start to change. The moment you let go and hang on to God, you'll see the sun break through. It's your brokenness that becomes your place of blessing.

If you've longed for the overcoming life, it starts with your surrender. Your present problems are not a curse from God, but the very instruments God is using to change you. *Your present problems are not God's punishment for your past mistakes but your opportunity to experience God more deeply.* You will wrestle with God over and over again in your life. You will wrestle over little things and big things. Each yes to God will bring you closer to freedom. Each yes will yield a harvest of fruitfulness. Each yes will set the foundation for the rest of your life. Each yes will bring you one step closer to home.

The normal Christian life is a lifelong journey of experiencing God's goodness on your hardest days and in your most devastatingly lonely nights. Someone once said that a faith that is not tried is a faith that is not true. If you're wrestling with God, you're about to experience God anew in your life. You're learning to die to yourself, and *that's* the normal Christian life.

When Jacob meets Esau, it's almost anticlimactic. By then Jacob is a new man. He's been transformed. He's been broken. He's in a place of absolute surrender. The brotherly reunion is an unexpectedly happy one. Esau leaves while Jacob lingers with his family, slowly making his way back home. But there was one more thing Jacob needed to do before calling it a day. After pitching his tent, Jacob built an altar. He called it El-Elohe-Israel meaning "God, the God of Israel."[1] Now his work was complete for the day. He could finally rest because he was home.

The boy who had started his journey tentatively receiving God's promises for him was now confident in the truth: God was his and he was God's. Identity. Security. Freedom. Rest. Jacob had found all that matters the most. Nothing could ever separate Jacob from his Father's love for him. His future was secure. His trust in God's goodness unshakeable.

Jacob had left home a boy but had finally returned home a man.

**SPEND A FEW MINUTES CONSIDERING THESE QUESTIONS, and bring your thoughts and feelings to God in prayer:**

*Have you ever felt stuck in an emotional wilderness?*

*Have you ever felt so overwhelmed by your faltering faith that you lost sight of God's presence in your life?*

*Do you understand that God's goodness is there for you?*

*Chapter 7*

# WHY CAN'T I FEEL MORE OF GOD IN MY LIFE?

Who would you want in the Intensive Care Unit with you if you had COVID-19 and were told you could have just one person in the room?

Don't overthink it. It's a theoretical question, but I'm asking it for a reason. Do you have the name of a person in mind yet? Your answer reveals a lot more about your relationships than you think. That person you picked to be with you during one of life's scariest experiences is the person that you most likely trust the most. It's the person you feel the safest with. It's the person you love.

All of us want to be with someone we love and trust when we're going through a difficult season. We want to be encouraged and supported. We want to feel loved. We want to know that someone has our back.

Which makes it immensely difficult to trudge through the normal Christian life without a deep sense of God's abiding presence. We want God in the room when we're struggling. In order for any of us to make it through the detours and delays and the obstacles and interruptions of the Christian life, we must learn to experience more of God in our lives. Yet most of us struggle with the same problem when it comes to God: we can't figure out why we can't see and feel more of God in our lives. No wonder we're discouraged. No wonder so many Christians want to quit.

If you find yourself drifting away from God and if your faith is slowly deconstructing, *nothing will propel you back into a thriving relationship with God faster than a clear manifestation of God's presence and power in your life.*

But how? How do we experience more of God in our normal suffering-filled, desire-laden Christian life? What stands in the way of our ability to experience God more fully?

My sister has a thing with red cardinals. Every time she sees one, she feels God is speaking to her. It's become a thing in our family. If you're having a bad day and see a red cardinal, we take a picture of it and share it with someone convinced it's a sure sign that God has opened the heavens and poured His favor on us. A few months after I moved into my new house, a cardinal and his mate built their nest in my backyard. I became convinced that God approved of my move. Does it sound hokey? Well, it might not be biblical, but I guarantee you, you'll think of God the next time you see a red cardinal.

You probably have your thing too. You feel God's presence more when you're alone in the mountains. Or you experience God more fully at the beach, or perhaps you sense Him most when you're singing worship songs at church. Someone in a small group was asked how they felt God's presence most in their life: "Whenever I read the Bible and my tears well up, I know God has spoken." We all have different ways of connecting with God.

But what happens when the tears don't come? What happens when you stop seeing red cardinals and all you feel is the ache of the burden you're carrying? What happens when you don't feel at all, when your soul becomes numb? Has God withdrawn His presence from you in those dry spells?

### God's Pleasure

I once went to a charismatic women's gathering in Australia with some friends. On the surface, the services were very much like mine. But the more I talked with people, the more I heard them describe experiences in the Christian life that I'd never experienced, despite having walked with the Lord for over twenty years at that time. They regularly saw God in their dreams. They heard God's voice audibly in their lives. They shared God stories I longed to have in my life too. Sensing my frustrations, they asked to pray for me. They willed me to experience their sort of personal revival and God experiences. I willed the earth to move and the heavens to shake all over me. Nothing happened. I went home disappointed and confused.

Phillip once felt the same frustration we experience when we long to see God, but can't. He begged Jesus: "Lord, show us the Father, and it is enough for us." Jesus rebuked Philip: "Have I been with you so long, and you still do not know me, Philip?" (John 14:8–9).

Much like Philip, we yearn for what is already ours. We long for what God has already given us in this normal Christian life. In our hunger and in our yearnings, we miss the obvious: God has already given us His full presence the moment we received Him into our hearts. In the words of the apostle Paul: "Or do you not realize this about yourselves, that Jesus Christ is in you?" (2 Cor. 13:5b).

In those moments when we thirst for the presence of God, we're usually not looking for an intellectual knowledge of God's presence. We're asking

> **Though we intellectually understand that the Christian life is a life of faith, our heart's desire is to live by sight and not by faith.**

for a manifestation of His presence in our lives. We want to experience God. We want to hear His voice. We want to see Him move. We want to receive His affirmation of "Well done, my beloved, in whom I am well pleased."

I suppose what we're looking for is proof. Though we intellectually understand that the Christian life is a life of faith, our heart's desire is to live by sight and not by faith. We want to be sure of this God we've never seen.

While our motivations and our desires are God-given and good, we fail in understanding *how* to experience God. Our very longings to see God, though noble—even holy sounding—often betray a misunderstanding of what true faith really is.

### Simon the Sorcerer

You and I aren't the first people to struggle with wanting to see more of God and His power in our lives. In Acts 8, the church was just starting to grow. The Spirit of God had come down at Pentecost with His awesome manifestation of power. Everyone was talking about God. The message of the gospel was spreading like wildfire despite heavy persecution. Lives were being transformed. Entire communities were giving their lives to Jesus. Christ's followers were living on mission, barely keeping up with the movement of the Spirit all around them.

One day Philip the disciple headed down to Samaria to preach the gospel. A revival broke out. People started giving their lives to Jesus and getting baptized. God was clearly at work. As was common in those early church days, miracles and supernatural signs were part of the movement of God.

Among the listening crowd was a man named Simon, a magician. In Luke's account of the story, we're told that, "Even Simon himself believed, and after being baptized he continued with Philip.

And seeing signs and great miracles performed, he was amazed" (Acts 8:13).

A few days later Peter and John showed up to help with the growing revival in Samaria. If God had moved before their arrival, their presence seemed to unleash the power of God in a fresh way. Wherever they laid their hands, fire came down. It was a whole new ballgame and Simon was in the proverbial bleachers watching the show. Whatever it was that Peter and John had, Simon wanted it too: "When Simon saw the Spirit was given through the laying on of the apostles' hands, he offered them money, saying, 'Give me this power also, so that anyone on whom I lay my hands may receive the Holy Spirit'" (vv. 18–19).

Peter must have seen past Simon's words straight to his heart and motives. His response to Simon sounds harsh and unforgiving no matter how many times I reread the story:

> "May your silver perish with you, because you thought you could obtain the gift of God with money! You have neither part nor lot in this matter, for your heart is not right before God. Repent, therefore, of this wickedness of yours, and pray to the Lord that, if possible, the intent of your heart may be forgiven you. For I see that you are in the gall of bitterness and in the bond of iniquity." (vv. 20–23)

Wow. Talk about putting someone in his place. Peter spared Simon no sorrow. Recognizing a sinful longing for personal power in Simon's heart, he boldly called him to repent. He didn't sugarcoat the truth because too much was at stake—Simon's soul was at stake.

What was it about Simon's desire that revealed the true colors of his heart?

Though Simon the sorcerer had received the message about Jesus and gotten baptized into the faith, it seems that was not enough for him. He longed for more. Whenever we long for more, we must slow down and figure out what we're longing for more of. It's not our longings *for more of* God that lead us away from God, it's our longings *for more from* God that deconstruct our faith.

Simon missed the truth about Christianity; in an effort to pursue God's power, he missed what we so often miss too—that Christianity is not the pursuit of God's abilities or power for ourselves but the pursuit of God Himself, working on our behalf through His power. God Himself is the breakthrough our souls were truly made to long for.

## Longing for Power

Our Christian culture is replete with Christians longing for "breakthrough." Simon wanted more of God's power in his life. He wanted a dramatic display of God's presence. Anything less would be considered lacking. Have you ever been to a church service where everyone around you seems to be moved by God in a much more dramatic way than you are? You can't help it. You feel like a failure. You want breakthrough too. You start to wonder about your faith. Questions clutter your mind: "Why doesn't God move in my life the same way He's moving in his? Why doesn't God answer my prayers like He's answering hers? Where is God when I need Him?" Questions turn to doubt, doubt turns to cynicism, cynicism turns to disbelief.

Why is it that we long for breakthroughs? What's behind our prayer to see more of God's power in our lives? Is it our faithlessness that places God on trial? Is it our self-centeredness that grows out of a sense of dissatisfaction in what God has given us? Or is it a genuine godliness that longs to lift the name of Jesus higher in our lives?

What is it that you desire the most in your Christian life? Is it a spiritual experience you long for or are you searching for the true and living God? How do you respond when you don't see God in manifest ways in your life? Is your faith strong enough to endure seasons of silence from God?

Sooner or later in the Christian life, most of us will struggle with God because we don't experience His presence and His voice in our lives daily in the way that we think we should. During those dry seasons, we crave even as little as a word from God.

Have you ever laid your baby or toddler down to sleep and stood on the other side of the door listening to that child cry, knowing you could go in and the child would stop, but choosing to wait because you know it's ultimately best for that child? Parents make difficult choices for their children during sleep training and other periods of raising them, but like the frustrated toddler, when it comes to my relationship with God, instead of settling down in understanding and trust, the absence of His reassuring voice has threatened to unravel me.

The psalmist understood God's intentional silences: "But I have calmed and quieted my soul, like a weaned child with its mother; like a weaned child is my soul within me" (Ps. 131:2).

If only I could consistently do the same.

### How Faith Unravels

The unraveling of my faith happened slowly for me, but by the time I noticed, God's silence was deafening.

I'd practiced Emergency Medicine for sixteen years when I was introduced to telemedicine. I remember the exhilaration I felt when I realized I could make a career out of telemedicine. I no longer had to be tied to one place. I quit the ER and became a teledoctor. I loved everything about it, but it consumed me.

I used to get up in the morning and spend an hour with God. I started this habit back in my early twenties and, despite a busy life, had stayed faithful to it. When I started seeing patients by phone, I told myself I didn't need to read my Bible first thing in the morning. I could see patients first. I told myself I could spend time with God in His Word later on in the day. I told myself that I could experience God anywhere, and not just in His Word. I could experience His presence in nature on a walk. I told myself that God was with me regardless. I basically lied to myself as, truly, I was not prioritizing my faith or time with Him. We all tell ourselves what we want to hear and call it the truth.

A week turned into a month turned into a year. I noticed that instead of reading my Bible "later" in the day, I had picked up a brand-new habit: I wasn't spending time with God at all. I assumed that God would understand. He'd given me a job that allowed me to help people while making a lot of money. His favor was on my life, and my heart was His after all.

Have you ever noticed how darkness comes slowly at dusk until the sun sets? It took a few months before I felt the utter darkness stifling my soul. I couldn't hear God anymore. I couldn't feel His presence in my life.

I was too proud to admit to myself that I had chosen money over God. I still wanted God's power and breakthrough, but I wanted it on *my* terms. I wanted God to still perform for me while I neglected the very activities that would draw me closer to His heart.

Something had to change.

### Broken

I once saw a toddler in the ER who could barely breathe. When I took a good look at the child, his color was ashen, his eyes sunken, his chest sucked in with the strain of breathing. "How long has he looked this color?" I asked his parents. They weren't sure. I checked the blood count, his hemoglobin was 3. (Normal is 15.) The child was admitted to the ICU and given blood transfusions to survive. He was dying and his parents hadn't even noticed. A review of his diet showed the cause. He was iron deficient. For months he had stopped eating iron-rich foods, his nutrition deteriorating to the point of near death.

This tragic event also serves as an analogy for what had happened to me. My soul was slowly dying, and I hadn't even noticed.

Sadly, it is what's happening in many of our churches today. Our souls are shriveling up, desperately anemic because of a poor intake of God's Word in our diets. In our longing to see God and experience breakthroughs, we have neglected to keep healthy on a steady diet of God's Word, one that securely leads us to His presence.

We've squeezed God out of our lives with our desire for money and status, distracted by our wants, surprised that we can't see God move in our lives anymore. We've sacrificed quiet moments with God, learning to hear His whisper, for an adrenaline-fueled arena filled with grandeur. We wonder why we don't experience more of God in our mundane daily lives. We've turned God into our personal genie in a bottle—asking Him for our own personal "spiritual experience" and becoming sullen and frustrated when God fails to deliver.

Like the dying toddler I took care of, we're dying spiritually and have barely noticed. We've looked for God in nature. We've looked for God in meditative poses. We've looked for God in life experiences. We've looked for God in every imaginable way except in the very place He's promised to be: in His Word. "In the beginning was the Word, and the Word was with God, and the Word was God" (John 1:1). Jesus, described in the gospel of John as the living Word of God, became flesh and dwelt among us. "Long ago, at many times and in many ways, God spoke to our fathers by the prophets, but in these last days he has spoken to us by his Son" (Heb. 1:1–2). But do you know how Jesus experienced the Father? He tells us exactly how in the gospel of Luke, chapter 24.

It's a few days after the crucifixion of Jesus when two disciples are walking despondently on the road to Emmaus. Their hearts are heavy with despair. Their faith in Jesus is slowly deconstructing. They had expected God to demonstrate His power over Caesar through Jesus the Messiah, not a dead man buried in a tomb. Jesus had massively disappointed them. Jesus, however, had bigger plans. Now resurrected, He ironically walks up right beside them. They're kept from recognizing the risen Christ at first. Jesus prods them to share their burden. They tell Him the entire story, then add these heart-wrenching words: "We had hoped that he [Jesus] was the one to redeem Israel" (v. 21). Jesus doesn't miss a beat. Instead of revealing Himself to them right then and there, He does a curious thing: "And beginning with Moses and all the Prophets, he interpreted to them in all the Scriptures the things concerning himself" (v. 27).

While the disciples on the road to Emmaus longed to see and experience the risen Messiah, Jesus simply opened God's Word and showed them the essence of His character and power and story and life and prophecy through the very Scriptures we ignore in our confusion and busyness. Later, the two disciples would comment on it: "Did not our hearts burn within us while he talked to us on the road, while he opened to us the Scriptures?" (v. 32).

Something remarkable, even divine, happens when we open God's inspired Word and look for Jesus. Our lives are transformed when we spend time in His Word. Breakthrough happens when we open the pages of Scripture and soak in the presence of God through it.

Do I sound like an old-fashioned preacher? Am I describing the same old practices you grew up being told you needed to do to maintain God's favor? Don't be fooled. Spending time with God through His Word might sound like an old practice, but it will yield fresh fruit in your life when you approach it with new rhythm. And it's not about earning His favor anyway. His grace is sufficient; it's about becoming aware of His presence in your life.

## Old Practices, New Rhythms

I was a Christian camp counselor as a young adult. Our camp director, Marty, would bring us in a week early and train us in helping kids through life's problems. I remember being petrified of not knowing what to tell a kid who asked a God-related question. Marty's goal was to give us the confidence to accurately convey the truth. He became well known for his persistent advice to any problem we ever lobbed him: "Read your Bible and pray." It became an inside joke, lovingly used by anyone who ever worked at that camp. Don't know what to wear today? Read your Bible and pray. Can't decide what to eat for lunch? Read your Bible and pray. Our entire Christian life was boiled down to these two time-tested practices. Read your Bible. Pray. If you did those two things, you were untouchable. In hindsight I'm sure his sentiment was somewhat tongue-in-cheek, but as a young person, I took it to heart.

I grew up in the church being taught the importance of old practices—better known as disciplines. Disciplines were cherished in my Lebanese Christian culture that valued hard work and rewarded good behavior. Read your Bible. Pray. Go to church on Sundays. Practice the Sabbath unless you're a doctor or a nurse. Memorize scripture. Journal. Fasting strongly advisable but excusable for the hypoglycemics among us.

Every one of those practices is good. Every one of those practices can lead to health. But practices that are rooted in duty instead of delight will choke your soul in time. It was happening to me. I got tired of reading my Bible. I got burned out praying about situations I didn't see get easily resolved. I never fasted, and I felt guilty about it. As an ER doctor I often worked on Sundays. I stunk at memorizing Scripture. No wonder I was frustrated in my faith. I felt guilty and overwhelmed.

It took a crisis for me to find God in His Word once again. It took a loneliness in my soul to awaken my thirst for God, a thirst that I was unable to quench no matter how hard I looked for ways to stop it.

## Light in the Darkness

It was a cold afternoon in late spring. In my pain, I felt isolated from everyone. I had no one to turn to. Even my therapist didn't seem to understand me. How had I gotten to this place? How had I become so alone? In my desolation, I saw the Bible on my coffee table. *Why even bother?* I wondered. I told myself it was a little too late to start reading my Bible now! And then simply because I had nothing left to say and nowhere else to look, I opened the Word of God randomly and I started reading:

> My God, My God, why have you forsaken me?
>> Why are you so far from saving me, from the words of my
>>> groaning?
> O my God, I cry by day, but you do not answer,
>> and by night, but I find no rest. . . .
>
> But I am a worm and not a man,
>> scorned by mankind and despised by the people.
> All who see me mock me;
>> they make mouths at me; they wag their heads;
> "He trusts in the Lord; let him deliver him;
>> let him rescue him, for he delights in him!" (Ps. 22:1–2, 6–8)

The words of Psalm 22 could have been taken out of my mouth.

I could feel the tears streaming down my face. I had looked for God in the success of my ministry. I had looked for God in the acceptance of my peers. I had looked for God in the comfort of my bank account. I had looked for God in nature and red cardinals. I had looked for God even in the presence of my therapist.

I had looked for God everywhere, but had finally found Him right where He had been all along: in the living pages of His Word.

Then it dawned on me as I read the words of the psalmist that those words weren't written about me at all. They were about Jesus. The very Savior I was wrestling with understood me completely. My very pain became the experience that brought me closer to His presence, that steadfast presence that had never left me.

I was experiencing breakthrough.

The very practices that had threatened to choke my soul became the saving graces in my life when I finally got to the place where I needed the Lord more than anything else in the world.

Rhythms are important to the Christian life. It's formulaic behavior that robs our souls of joy. Rhythms that are rooted in relationship are life-giving. My parents would drink Turkish coffee together every morning before my dad left for work and every evening upon his return. They maintained this rhythm through forty-seven years of marriage. Soul nourishing rhythms are rooted in delight. The more we delight in Jesus, the more those old-fashioned rhythms give meaning to our lives.

When the love of God and the assurance of His presence filled my heart again, Bible reading became the means to hear God's voice. Prayer became my opportunity to pour out my soul to Him, my willingness to become vulnerable and open with the lover of my soul. Though the Sabbath is still a struggle in my work-obsessed nature, I'm slowly learning to let go and trust the Lord with my life more. And fasting . . . well, we all grow in stages.

Is it wrong to ask God to show Himself mightily in our lives? Is it wrong to look for a breakthrough? I'm glad you asked! No, I don't believe it's wrong to want to see God and experience Him more fully. I don't believe it's wrong to ask for obvious manifestations of God or to beg for seasons of breakthrough. I don't believe God is unable to reveal His ways through your circumstances or other people's words or even red cardinals.

There's a peculiar account in Isaiah 7:11–14. Ahaz is the king of Judah when the Lord speaks to him: "Ask a sign of the LORD your God; let it be deep as Sheol or high as heaven." Ahaz tries to outsmart God: "I will not ask, and I will not put the LORD to the test." God wasn't impressed: "Hear then, O house of David! Is it too little for you to weary men, that you weary my God also? Therefore the Lord himself will give you a sign. Behold, the virgin shall conceive and bear a son, and shall call his name Immanuel."

Instead of commending Ahaz, God rebuked him for not showing trust in asking God for a sign. The point is that it's okay to ask for a sign of God's presence. Looking for God's presence through signs and asking for breakthrough is not evil. It's good. But judging God's goodness by whether or not He delivers when we ask is arrogant at best.

The key is to learn to let go of the formulas we rely on to try to manipulate God's power. The key is to rest in the truth undergirded by God's love for us. Faith comes by hearing and hearing by the word of God. *Faith trusts God, and when it's shaken, faith rests its feet on God's Word.*

There are seasons in life when God speaks loudly and seasons where He is silent. There are seasons in life for signs and breakthroughs and seasons for delays and denials. There are seasons for answers to prayer requests and seasons for striving in prayer.

The Christian life is all about rhythms. These rhythms become holy when they are centered on the person of Christ and the character of God. There is a rhythm to silence and solitude—sometimes practiced in the wilderness alone, and other times stolen in quiet moments, surrounded by a crowd. There is a rhythm to prayer—sometimes we groan, other times we whisper, and at times we shout

out to the Lord. There is a rhythm to fasting. There is a rhythm to fellowship with other believers. There is a rhythm to reading God's Word; sometimes we read entire books at a time, other times we rest in the depth of one verse. There is even a rhythm to asking for signs; sometimes God wants us to ask for signs, other times He asks us to trust Him without them.

*The goal of Christian rhythm is to deepen our knowledge of God and become more familiar with His character and with His works.* This kind of soul-deepening work can't be rushed. While you might turn off your radio and shut down your computer, it takes time to cultivate silence in your soul. It takes time to learn to hear the whisper of your Father. But it's work that's needed if you long to experience the presence of God more deeply in your life. Most of us don't hear God's voice because we're too distracted to hear it.

> **The goal of Christian rhythm is to deepen our knowledge of God and become more familiar with His character and with His works.**

Dallas Willard once said: "Hurry is the great enemy of spiritual life in our day. You must ruthlessly eliminate hurry from your life."[1] This kind of work takes time.

Do you know God? Are you becoming more familiar with His character and His works? Are you hedging your life on His goodness or are you leery of His silences? Do you trust God's goodness in your suffering? Do you trust Him enough to bring Him all of your desires? Do you trust Him enough to let go of your hurt? Do you long for God or are you just after His power?

You might have convinced yourself that if you could just experience a more tangible presence of God in your life, you would change.

You might have convinced yourself that your faith crisis would resolve if God would just . . . *do* something!

He already has, beginning the day you first chose to trust Him. He's given you His life. He's given you Himself.

What if instead of straining to see more of God's power, you simply asked Him to help you be quiet enough to hear His whisper, then discipline yourself to do so? What if instead of trudging through old practices, you chose to practice new rhythms?

God might still surprise you. You might just look up and see that there's a red cardinal perched on that tree, or you might not, because it's not a sign you're counting on to assure you of God's nearness.

And when you're stuck in the ICU struggling to take your next breath, you'll know that only one person will do. His name is Jesus.

**SPEND A FEW MINUTES CONSIDERING THESE QUESTIONS,**
**and bring your thoughts and feelings to God in prayer:**

*How do you respond when you don't see God in manifest ways in your life?*

*Is your faith strong enough to endure seasons of silence from God?*

*Can you hear God's whisper?*

*What do you want to say to God about this, now?*

*Chapter 8*

# WHY IS IT HARD FOR CHRISTIANS TO LOVE?

I love going to Lebanon, but I hate flying there.

I can tell the minute I walk up to the gate at the airport headed to Beirut that I'm not in Kansas anymore. I can tell by the smell. I can tell by the tone of voices around me. I can tell by the hijabs. I can tell because they're my people, and we're not always known for our finesse.

And if there is anything worse than sitting uncomfortably at the gate with a bunch of my people, try sitting on a plane in a row next to a few of us. It's the worst. We're loud. We're messy. We're difficult. My solution is that I fake it. From the moment I walk up to the gate until I get into the cab leaving the Beirut International Airport, I act like I am an American. I don't speak Arabic. I don't look people in the eyes. I am all American all the way home.

Many Christians suffer the same plight in real life. We act as if our time in this world is like those four hours en route to Lebanon. We dread the times we rub shoulders with the others. We hate the ways of the world, the loudness of our people, even their smells. We act like we're different or better than the others. We step out from time to time to "serve" the lowly people but we hurry back to the safety of our homes. We feed the hungry, tend to wounds, check off our lists feeling good about ourselves, all the while convinced that we are better, even if through God's grace.

No wonder Christians have failed so many.

One day as I sat in my seat on the British Airways flight leaving Lebanon with "the others," I looked across the aisle and saw a very old woman pull out a big Bible. That thing weighed at least ten pounds. Her English voice carried all the way across the aisle to my seat even though her face was turned toward the guy in the middle seat. She was explaining how she had spent the last twenty years in Beirut ministering to Arabs and was moving back home because of her age. This had not been an easy decision for her given how much she loved the people, my people. The more excited she became, the more the pages of her Bible rustled, the many tiny little sticky notes slipping out. I could see the pages of her Bible underlined in many colors. She never stopped talking to the man the entire flight to London. I finally dared peek at the man, expecting to see annoyance and dismay. Instead, what I saw took my breath away—he was smiling. His eyes reflecting what he knew to be true—he was loved.

The old English lady had not tried to "save" the man. She had not ignored him, and she hadn't tried to change him. All she did was humbly share the story of Jesus with him. She was simply there to love him.

I was witnessing what it means to be set apart, and I repented. I repented of my impatience and my self-righteousness. I repented of the hardness of my heart. I repented of missing who my Father really is—a God of unconditional love and grace and compassion.

You might be reading this chapter because you've been hurt by the church. You've felt shunned by the church. You have not been loved well. The church might have failed you, but Christ's love never will. *Just because people let you down, don't give up on the God who never will.*

I am not one to gloss over the truth. I believe God's Word to be true—every bit of it. I believe in God's sovereign power to save people. I believe in the Holy Spirit's ability to convict us and change us. I believe in God's goodness that calls us to repentance. I believe in God's desire to purify the church. I believe God's will is to save the perishing. And I believe God is big enough to do the work of God in both believing and unbelieving people.

I also believe in love. I believe in God's unconditional and steadfast love for me and for you. I believe in His love that beckons me home when I'm struggling. I believe in His love that waits patiently for me to change when I'm resisting. I believe in God's love that doesn't ignore truth but loves me enough to draw me to His truth. And I believe in His same love for you!

> **God's Word *is* the truth that pierces us, and His love is the power that changes us.**

It's hard to love in the way of Jesus. We struggle to love difficult people. We struggle to love people who don't seem to change. We struggle to love people who have hurt us before. We struggle in setting the right boundaries. We struggle with loving people without constantly needing to persuade them of the truth.

It's not *either* truth *or* love, it's always *both* truth *and* love. God's Word *is* the truth that pierces us, and His love is the power that changes us.

One of my best friends is a lesbian; that might not be a big deal to everyone reading this, but for more conservative Christians like me, it's something! I met Sarah in the ER shortly after she was hired as a tech. Sarah was gay; she was out and proud. Even my somewhat oblivious mom would have picked up on Sarah's sexual orientation.

I liked her from the start, and it didn't take long for Sarah and me to become good friends. Sarah laughed at my jokes. She kept up with my pace, and she agreed with my sentiments on most issues in life. I barely noticed in those early days of friendship that she had been studying me carefully. By then I was already knee deep in the ministry and had a solid online presence which made my conservative biblical beliefs very public and open to scrutiny.

I later would find out that Sarah was hanging with me by day and watching my YouTube channel by night. Eventually, she received Jesus as her personal Savior. It came during an especially difficult trial in her life. She stepped right into the arms of the Savior who had given His life for her. Shortly after receiving Jesus, she married her girlfriend. She didn't invite me to the wedding.

We were the odd couple in the ER: "the Jesus-loving doctor and the Jesus-loving homo" (Sarah's words, not mine). No one could figure it out. No one still can. But our friendship grew. When my dad died, my pain was too deep for words. Sarah was one of only three of my friends who showed up to the funeral. I'll forever be grateful for her presence in my life during that time.

After her marriage ended, I figured Sarah had grown enough in her understanding of the Scriptures to finally see that God might be offering her an opportunity to leave her sinful lifestyle. Instead, she fell in love with another woman who used to be married to a man and is co-habitating with her to this day.

Sarah recently asked me if I regretted the fact that despite my discipling her for so many years, she is still gay. I answered truthfully: no, I had no regret. But that wasn't always the case. For the longest time, I felt torn. Was Sarah a "true believer," or was she lying to herself about what she called the Christian faith? Had she really received Jesus while continuing to love a woman? I read articles affirming both sides of the matter, and I remained convinced that God's plan for marriage was between one man and one woman. I reassured myself that only God knew the heart. I became frustrated with the Lord over the matter. Why wasn't He changing her? Until one day, worn out, I realized that this was a burden I no longer needed to carry.

Sarah is God's child. She is His business. I am just the friend. My role is to love her, not to fix her.

We live in a postmodern culture that defines truth as subjective and love as tolerance. Christians feel stuck between a rock and a hard place: Do we lead with truth, harping down on what God's Word says, or do we choose to love, diminishing biblical principles on holy living? It doesn't have to be either/or. One of the most relevant and hardest verses for me to live out in our world is Ephesians 4:15 which directs us to "speak the truth in love."

Christian author Warren Wiersbe once said that "truth without love is brutality and love without truth is hypocrisy."[1] The church has been guilty of choosing one side or another: truth without love versus love without truth. A balanced approach, or rather a Christ-like approach, is needed.

> **When it comes to love, the conservative evangelical church has been tried by the secular culture and found failing.**

I understand that many young people have no energy left for extremes. Many hold the notion that evangelical Christians are fundamentally judgmental. Many believe biblical Christianity to be intolerant and unloving. Unwilling to throw the baby out with the bathwater, some Christians have continued to hold on to Jesus while abandoning evangelical Christianity. Other Christians have continued to hold on to Jesus while re-creating their own interpretation of orthodox biblical viewpoints. Some Christians continue to sit in evangelical pews, but their list of questions is growing and they wonder whether they even belong there.

When it comes to love, the conservative evangelical church has been tried by the secular culture and found failing. The seeming lack of love in the church is not always restricted to the LGBTQ+ community. The church has also failed to love Muslims, immigrants, divorced people, victims of abuse, women, minorities, single moms, and others. The list goes on and on. In John 13:35, Jesus told us that "by this all people will know that you are my disciples, if you have love for one another," so why are so many Christians known for what they hate or reject?

Why is it so hard for Christians to love? Maybe, for some of us, it's that we have believed the lie that to love someone is synonymous with condoning their behavior. It's not. We have believed the lie that we have only two choices when it comes to how we treat those we don't agree with: tolerance or lack of tolerance. And sadly, this lie we have believed comes from the world and not the Bible. But there is another way. It's the way of Jesus, who IS love.

Jesus was known to be a friend of sinners. He was accused of hanging out with prostitutes and tax collectors and of partying too much. Instead of loudly denying the rumors, Jesus continued to love. His life revealed the truth: Jesus did not condone sin. He called it out—all of it, including religious hypocrisy. He didn't indulge in sin. He victoriously fought against it. Jesus sat with sinners, but He was set apart from sinners. Jesus stuck out in His culture *because* He made an impression. He was different from everyone else, but He loved everyone else. He was set apart in His attitudes; He was set apart in His love.

My friendship with Sarah has taught us both about Christian relationship and love, as we both try to live lives that align with our faith. Yes, we're different. No, we don't agree on everything in the Bible, and we are both very clear on that, but year by year, I am learning more about stepping away from the so-called culture wars and keeping my gaze on Jesus.

## Set Apart

The concept of being set apart is designed by God. It is not a call to be isolated or unwelcoming. It is a call to be holy. It is a call to reflect who God is. It is a call rooted in love and intended to reflect true love. It takes courage to do both—to be set apart without isolating. When God calls His people to be set apart, He's not calling them to keep others out but to invite others in.

The people of Israel longed to fit into the world around them. Their story started out when God called Abraham to leave his home and follow the one true God. In a world that believed in many gods, Abraham's God was radical. This was a God who cared. This living God made a covenant with Abraham. He promised Abraham a family, a land, and the eventual birth of the Savior through his line. Abraham's family grew and settled in Egypt. They lived there for four hundred years under the oppressive hand of Pharaoh. When they became tired and worn out, they cried out to God. God saved them. He gave them a breakthrough.

God then led the people of Israel out of Egypt powerfully and magnificently. He took them to Mount Sinai where they saw His power and glory. They were given His laws. The people of Israel weren't perfect. Even in those days of early freedom, like us, they broke God's rules, they grumbled and complained, they argued and were tempted to worship false idols and gods. They experienced God's judgment for their sin, but they also experienced God's grace regularly in those wandering years. God was leading them to freedom. He was committed to them. He led them to the promised land.

And then they lived happily ever after worshiping their God who had led them to this lush land.

Wrong!

The people of Israel had barely settled into the promised land when they began to grumble. They wanted a king. The reason was simple: they didn't trust God. In fact, their request for a king upset the prophet Samuel. But God told Samuel to do as the people wanted because they had rejected Him from being king over them (1 Sam. 8:6–7). They wanted to fit in with the rest of the world.

They didn't understand that to be set apart was a gift, not a curse. That to be set apart testified of their unique history and their God. To be set apart was their power in a world where everyone was the same. They didn't want to feel like outsiders. They didn't want to be different. So, in 1 Samuel 8, they asked God for a king.

No one wants to be different. When I moved from Beirut to Green Bay as a fifteen-year-old, I was clearly different and I hated it. I wanted to fit in. I tried to speak like everyone else and failed. I tried to dress like everyone else and have pictures from the '80s to prove it. I even got a perm.

I missed that my strength came from my differences. I missed that it was those very things that set me apart that would open doors for me and pave the way to the future. I missed that behaving like everyone else did not fix my identity problem. It just masked it.

Still . . . God gave the people of Israel a king with a warning: they would live to regret their decision. And they did.

The people of Israel immediately regretted their decision the moment they understood what it looked like to be the servants of a human king. They regretted it when they were ruled by evil kings for generations to come. They continued to regret it when their people split into two nations, Judah and Israel, and after their exile to Babylon.

It took a few centuries, but in due time, Jesus came and changed everything.

## Some Good News

The New Testament begins four hundred years after the Old. The people of Israel were still longing for a king. This time, their King came in a manger. He wasn't riding on a stallion. Instead of ruling the world with an iron fist, He cradled it with love. Instead of reigning over the world in victory, He was crucified by the world on a tree.

It was Christ's death and resurrection that made a way for a new kingdom to be born and a new rule to be established.

This would be a kingdom set apart from the world. This kingdom would be different from anything else anyone had experienced so far. It would be a kingdom born of love. And anyone who claimed this kingdom would also be called to be set apart by love. In the words of Jesus:

"If you were of the world, the world would love you as its own; but because you are not of the world, but I chose you out of the world, therefore the world hates you." (John 15:19)

"I do not ask that you take them out of the world, but that you keep them from the evil one. They are not of the world, just as I am not of the world." (17:15–16)

Christ's call for us to be set apart has never been about pushing a political or religious agenda, nor is it a call to promote a haughty self-righteous "we're better than everyone else" way. His call for us to be set apart is not about judgment. Christ's call for us to be set apart has always been a call to be like Him. It's a call to mercy and compassion, a call to self-sacrifice in a culture familiar with fighting for self. The call to be set apart is a call to the cross where we willingly die to self for the sake of others.

The message of salvation has never been based on people's ability to change in order to fit into God's kingdom. Rather, Christ invites us to His kingdom where we're welcomed in love and can't help but change. When the Pharisees grumbled about Christ eating with tax collectors and sinners, Jesus told them the truth: "Those who are well have no need of a physician, but those who are sick. I came not to call the righteous, but sinners" (Mark 2:17).

In other words, Christ didn't come to save one particularly bad group of sinners. Rather, He came to save all sinners as long as they recognize the need to be saved and forgiven for their sins. It's good news because it's mine, and it's yours. The gospel is good news because it does not hinge on my changing first, but invites me into the kingdom with the promise of helping me change, heal, and become more like Christ every day.

And, oh, how I need to change. I need to have more patience in a world that is rushed. I need more kindness in a world that is harsh. I need more love in a world full of hate. I need more forgiveness in a world that holds grudges. I need more reconciliation in a world that's broken. I need more hope in a world of despair. I need more holiness in a world that is sullied.

### Holy, Holy, Holy

What does it mean to be holy?

We've spent a lot of time talking about the goodness of God. Equally important is another attribute of God: He is holy. That God is holy means that He is absolutely separate from and exalted above all His creatures and creation, and He is entirely separate from all moral evil and sin. In Leviticus 19:2 Moses speaks God's words to the people of Israel: "Speak to all the congregation of the people of Israel and say to them, You shall be holy, for I the LORD your God am holy." Peter reiterated the call to holiness in his letter: "since it is written, 'You shall be holy, for I am holy'" (1 Peter 1:16).

Holiness is God's expectation for His followers.

But how do I live holy in a complicated, busy, secular world? How do I become separate from evil and sin to stand before a Holy

God? The answer has always been and will always be Jesus Christ. Jesus paid the price so that I could stand holy before a Holy God. It is only because of the death and resurrection of the Son of God that we are called holy as His followers.

It turns out that our holiness, our striving to live set apart, devoted to a holy God, is not only an act of obedience to our holy God, but is also an act of love for those who do not yet know this God. We are the sweet-smelling aroma of God to those who are perishing (2 Cor. 2:15). Love doesn't demolish the truth of the gospel and God's Word or minimize its power. Love paves the way for others to hear the truth and maximizes its impact.

### Finding Love at Church

I was the main speaker at an event at a conservative church recently. I waited on the front row, alone, while a trickle of women filed in. Two twenty-something women with dreadlocks and more body piercings than I could count walked right up to me and sat in the empty row behind me. They didn't look like "typical church girls."

I was immediately intrigued.

When one of them stepped out for a minute, I couldn't help myself. I turned back and struck up a conversation with the other.

"Is that your sister?" I asked.

"No. She's my girlfriend."

I was even *more* intrigued.

"Tell me your story," I prodded.

She told me how she had met her girlfriend via the internet and started a long-distance relationship. She told me how she moved from Florida to Chicago to be with her girlfriend, a mother of four. She told me how, after she moved, she looked for a church and found one that sounded in name close to the one she used to go to in Florida. I asked if she'd cared that the church was not affirming of her lifestyle. She assured me she did not. Her response surprised me. She explained:

"I felt the spirit of God here, so I came."

"Weren't you uncomfortable, wondering if you were being judged?"

"Not at all. I could tell that they loved me just the way I am and that was more important to me than anything else. I knew God was here from the way that they loved me."

I thought about my friend Sarah. For some time, I'd worried about whether my friendship with her sent mixed signals to others about what I believed to be true in God's Word. I worried about my own sinfulness and hypocrisy, judging Sarah. I worried about a whole lot of things.

And then it dawned on me.

God had not called me to change Sarah. That's God's job, not mine! God had not called me to condemn Sarah. God had not called me even to worry about Sarah. He had simply called me to love her. Having clearly shared God's Word with her, I could now release her, trusting in His love for Sarah, and trusting that it's the Spirit's role to convict us of sin. With His Word, He could teach her. All He wanted me to do was to love her, just like the church I was sitting in had loved the lesbian couple who were anxiously waiting to hear me teach God's Word. They weren't expecting me to water down the message of the gospel. They were expecting the truth.

In that instance, I got a glimpse of what it means to be set apart.

Yet balancing truth and love is not as easy as it sounds for most of us, is it?

## Love Always Wins

The world has never been more connected than it is now. We have the ability through technology to reach the world like never before.

Instead of wasting our days judging all the people who don't believe the same things we do, we could just love them. Mother Teresa is attributed with saying: "If you judge people, you have no time to love them."[2]

Ironically, when my church world was falling apart and I was leery of God's people, it was God's people who ended up saving me. I stumbled my way into Christians who saw past my defenses. They didn't run when I bristled. They didn't ask questions when I wasn't ready for them. They didn't ask me to explain myself, nor did they ask me to defend my choices. They didn't lay down ultimatums. They didn't even ask me to change. They just saw through my hurt and chose to love me, nevertheless. Perhaps their strength came from their ability to clearly discern God's whispers in their lives. Perhaps their love grew out of their own past wounds now healed by God's steadfast and unconditional love for them.

Though my former church had been the cause of so much of my pain, the church also became the place where I found healing from my pain.

It's not easy to love the leery, the bristled, the hurting the way Jesus does. We risk getting hurt when we love unconditionally. We risk getting misunderstood when we love like Jesus loved. But it's a risk worth taking, not for the hope of our own acceptance, but for their understanding.

You might still be struggling in your faith. You might still have more questions than answers. You might still be straining to hear the Savior's voice. God's voice has a way of becoming clearer when one of His children takes your hand in theirs and walks with you toward the Savior who is still waiting to welcome home His prodigal child.

Just ask my friend Sarah.

Sometimes, finding your way back to God starts when you stumble your way into God's people.

**SPEND A FEW MINUTES CONSIDERING THESE QUESTIONS,**
**and bring your thoughts and feelings to God in prayer:**

*Who is hard for me to love?*

*When have I shied away from loving someone difficult or
different from me?*

*Can I ask God to fill my heart with love today?*

*Chapter 9*

# IS IT SUPPOSED
# TO BE *THIS* HARD?

I almost quit the faith once. It did not happen at the beginning of my journey as a believer. It happened in the middle.

The mess is always in the middle.

I'm a middle child, so I can attest to that fact. It's easy and exciting to start. Firstborns are a novelty. They're exciting and fun. And if you're the baby, you're like that last bite of ice cream after a delicious meal. Everyone wants to savor the very last bite. It's the middle child who tends to be the problem. Many of us who are middle children are trouble with a capital T. We're unexpected and willful. We've got a mind of our own and we're difficult to control. Like I said, the mess is always in the middle.

Likewise, most of the significant issues in the Christian life don't rear themselves in the early stages. They develop over time. New believers experience what the Bible calls our first love (Rev. 2:4). There is a fresh awareness of all that God has done for us. There is deep joy over our forgiveness and the promise of eternal life with our maker. Our lives take on a lighter note immediately following our understanding of God's love for us.

It's in the middle that the Christian life most often becomes hard.

When I started walking with Jesus, I never imagined that I would ever be tempted to quit the faith. I assumed that if I started well and did all the right things, life in Christ would be smooth sailing, or at the very least more joyful at any future points than times in the past. You know my story well by now. Life is never as easy as we wish it would be.

Over the years I've wanted to quit my church. I've wanted to quit my small group. I've wanted to quit my ministry. And, yes, it happened to me in the middle.

Today I'm walking in faith again. I am trusting in God's goodness even though I don't have all the answers yet. I am confident that I am God's, and He is mine. I still have occasional questions, but I know who to go to for answers. I still have some days where I struggle with Christians, and I have to remind myself that I'm safe in the church. I still have days where I wonder about God's ways, but I no longer think about quitting.

When you picked up this book, you had questions. You likely had doubts about God and about Christianity. Maybe your story is similar to mine with loads of church hurt in your past. Or maybe your pain is related to hypocrisy in your home or disappointment in your life. I hope by now you see that your faith does not have to end in deconstruction. I hope by now you see that the deconstructing of your faith can lead to the rebuilding of it. You are not stuck in your painful circumstances. Your suffering is not a slammed door but instead is God's pathway for your purpose. Your God-given desires are indeed holy—don't minimize them or ignore them. Your pain won't always rule your life. As you release it, you will always find that God is stronger than the pain that's been inflicted on you. You *can* hear God's voice. You *can* rest assured in His presence. You don't have to quit in the middle. You can make it to the end.

### Been There, Done That

We are not the first people who have been tempted to quit in the middle.

I've always been a fan of Mark (sometimes called John Mark), the author of the second gospel in the New Testament. He was just a boy at the time that Jesus lived and died. He grew up in a faithful, religious family. His uncle Barnabas was famous in the early church for his leadership and generosity. Mark gave his life to Christ early on and was soon invited to join the great apostle Paul and uncle Barnabas on their first missionary journey. What an opportunity! What a destiny this young man was given.

The only problem is that halfway through the journey, Mark quit (Acts 13). He had had enough. He was okay at the start, but he hit some turbulence in the middle, and mistook it for the end, so he bailed. The Christian life wasn't all he expected it to be.

Was the road too uncomfortable for his comfort? Was he tired of living in the shadow of Paul and Barnabas? Was he disillusioned by the persecution that he faced when he'd been expecting applause instead? It was big news in the church when Mark split. It hurt the church that he left. Paul was so bothered by Mark's "deconstruction" that he had a fallout with Barnabas over it.

In Acts 15:37–39 we're told: "Now Barnabas wanted to take with them John called Mark. But Paul thought best not to take with them one who had withdrawn from them in Pamphylia and had not gone with them to the work. And there arose a sharp disagreement, so that they separated from each other."

*Ouch.*

Barnabas wanted to give Mark a second chance. Paul wasn't ready for that. I wonder how Mark responded. Did it hurt him to hear Paul's response? Did he ask God to vindicate his name? Did he isolate from others to nurse his wounds and a broken ego?

But God wasn't through with Mark. Does it surprise you that God is a God of second chances? I've noticed that I give less grace for myself than God is willing to grant me. It's not that God lets me get away with sin, but He is longsuffering and patient with me, drawing me to repentance. He waits for me to see the light. He extends mercy to me when I'm giving myself a lecture and a kick in the rear. Where I expect myself to behave perfectly, God already knows that I'm never going to get it perfectly right. He didn't save me because of my future potential. He saved me despite my future potential. He didn't promise to love me if I performed consistently well. He loved me while I was a sinner still in need of His grace. He isn't holding His breath hoping I turn out to be worth the investment He's made in me. Rather, He takes joy in extending His kingdom to me and allowing me to be used for His glory.

God is a God of second chances, and God had more plans for Mark despite the fact that Mark had quit.

In 2 Timothy 4:11, Paul was in prison in what is thought to be the last chapter of his life before dying. In his concluding letter to the church, Paul wrote these words: "Get Mark and bring him with you, for he is very useful to me for ministry."

Somewhere past the mess in the middle, Mark's faith had slowly reconstructed. Somewhere past the mess in the middle, Mark was back in the game. What was it that turned him back to his calling? Was it the love of an uncle who never gave up on him? Was it God's mercy that woke him up to God's presence? Was it Peter who helped Mark by taking him under his wings? It's believed that the gospel according to Mark was written by Mark but heavily influenced by Peter, which means that not only did Mark's faith get built up again, but God still had big plans for this young man.

God still has big plans for you! The Christian life won't get any easier. People will still disappoint you, including Christians. The suffering in your life won't stop. Odds are you'll be hurt again, but if you're a child of God, your future is untouchable, your destiny is secure. You've been welcomed back, just like Mark was.

### Not Everyone Finishes Well

The same could not be said of Demas.

We don't know a lot about Demas, but we know enough. In Philemon 24, Paul describes Demas as a fellow worker. In Colossians 4:14, Paul again writes about Demas, a fellow laborer in Christ, "Luke the beloved physician greets you, as does Demas." Paul and Luke and Demas were thought to be in a prison in Rome when Paul wrote these words. In those days, Demas was still following hard after Jesus.

And then somewhere in the middle, something shifted. Was it a hurt that Demas suffered? Was it an expectation that remained unmet? Was it a question without an answer, a seed of doubt, confusion, uncertainty, or a sense of God's absence? Or was it just desire, a longing for more, a hope that God would do more for him that never materialized? Whatever the cause was, Paul summed it up in 2 Timothy 4:9–10: "Do your best to come to me soon. For Demas, in love with this present world, has deserted me and gone to Thessalonica."

This man of faith who had spent a lifetime with Paul suffering for the sake of Jesus had lost his moorings in the middle. He chose Thessalonica instead—the city on the water, a place of prominence and comfortable entertainment. Safety. Ease. Freedom from God's uncommon ways. In the middle of the road, Demas had had enough. He stopped believing God. He decided to quit working so hard. Life could be better outside of the church. Life made more sense without God's people. Somewhere in the middle, Demas concluded: "It's not supposed to be this hard."

What has you thinking about forsaking the Lord? Is it your longing for intimacy, a happy marriage, the pull of what the world has to offer? Is it your desire for a bigger house, a better job, more savings, success? Is it the struggle between who you see yourself to be that doesn't quite match who God's Word says you should be? Are you tired, worn out, frustrated that no matter how hard you've tried to do the right things, you're still dissatisfied with Christianity? You're not happy. You're not changing. You can't feel God. You still dislike His people.

You've had enough. You show little fruit for your sacrifice.

Elijah felt it once, too, and he became suicidal.

Jeremiah complained to God about the same thing more than once.

Job went through a hellish experience and reached the same conclusions. He wrote an entire book bemoaning his life and his faith.

King Saul felt it too. Tired of waiting on God, his is a story like Demas's. He quit in the middle and never made it back home.

> **We can't ignore the extent God will go to reach us. We forget the cross where Jesus laid down His life for us so that we might live.**

Most Christians forget what the gospel message really is. We forget how deeply God loves us. We forget how accepted we are. We forget that we belong. We forget that we can't eradicate the power of God's love. We can't ignore the extent God will go to reach us. We forget the cross where Jesus laid down His life for us so that we might live.

This book is about remembering. It's about remembering that we are loved—whether we believe it or not. Remembering that we are chosen even when we fail. It's a book about remembering that it's God's goodness that holds on to us when we can't hold on anymore.

Sometimes, you have to reach your lowest in order to find out what's true: that God loves you and that nothing will ever separate you from the love of God. That as you drag your way back home—fearful of the price you're going to have to pay for leaving, battered and worn out and aged and sorrowful—the last face you expect to see is the tear-drenched face of your Father who never stopped waiting for you to come home.

I'd always thought of myself as the older brother in the story of the prodigal. I lived by the rules; I didn't cause trouble. I looked obedient to outside appearances. Like the older brother, I worked so hard, and felt nobody noticed. Like the older brother I started to resent the Father. Didn't He see all the hard work I did for Him? Why wasn't He rewarding me for my efforts? Like the older brother, I missed that my Father's presence was the fruit to be enjoyed, that unhindered fellowship with my Father was the source of my comfort.

> **The grace of God is manifested in that moment in the pigsty when you finally realize that the worst life in your Father's house will always exceed the best life away from His presence.**

But somewhere in the middle, I jumped ship. I wandered from home. I quit going to church. I landed in a pigsty. When I came to my senses, I saw that I was much more like the prodigal. I'd turned my heart from my Father's love. I took what I could and I ran. I flirted with the world like Demas before me. I yearned for its accolades. I longed for its successes and recognition. I envied those who had what I wanted. And I almost sold everything to get it, including my soul in the process.

*The grace of God is manifested in that moment in the pigsty when you finally realize that the worst life in your Father's house will always exceed the best life away from His presence.*

God's grace is that moment when you hear a whisper in your heart, the whisper that beckons you to come home. And God's grace is manifested in that moment of reckoning when you understand that it's time to go back home.

## Finding My Way Home

I hadn't made it to church in six months. Hardly anybody noticed. I hid it with my travel schedule and my professional responsibilities at the hospital. My life sounded noble, but I was drifting. I was hurting. My soul was parched for God. I felt dislocated and unanchored. I had talked to my counselor about it, and the pastor at my new church had caught on to my ways, but he hadn't pressed me on the matter.

One day, a friend I respect emailed to invite me to join a Christian writers' group. I was thrilled, as many of the writers in that group were people I admired. A couple of days later, she emailed me again with a condition: "The board wants to know where you stand on the church thing, given your history with church hurt. Are you part of a local church?"

Some things don't make much sense to others, but that was my moment of reckoning, my moment of grace. I can't explain to you why that encounter was the tipping point to cause me to get out of the pigsty and start making my way back home, but it was the nudge that I needed to settle the matter. I hadn't found answers outside of the church. My heart was tethered to the God I was wrestling with. I was too tired to do anything but let go.

And just as clear as I could hear it, God's whisper came through to my thick head: "Will you just say yes to Me on this?"

Just say yes—it was all God was asking me to do. Just say yes. It was such a small thing in the big scheme of my life, a quiet whisper where I was hoping for a tsunami. But if you've ever heard God's whisper, it's an unmistakable thing.

The Christian life usually boils down to your yeses. From the moment of salvation, God stands at the door of your heart knocking.

Only you can open the door. Only you can take that one step. Only you can say yes to God. He doesn't tear the door down. He won't send in the National Guard. It's always been just between you and God. It's just one word that flows out of a heart that trusts God but it will change the course of your life.

Demas said no to God and became a footnote in the life of Paul.

Mark said yes to God and he ended up writing a gospel.

We tend to complicate the Christian life. We overthink surrender. We look for signs. We wait and gesticulate while the Christian life really boils down to one word: yes.

Yes, God, I'll forgive the person who hurt me.

Yes, God, I'll let go of my anger.

Yes, God, I'll go to church again.

Yes, God, I'll trust You in the waiting.

Yes, God, I'll throw away that bag of "marshmallows."

Yes, God, I'll do whatever You ask me to.

Your future depends on your willingness to say yes to God, and your yes hinges on your belief in the goodness of God. Understanding the goodness of God depends upon first knowing it through the Holy Scriptures. When the prodigal came to his senses, he was counting on the goodness of his father.

### Let's Talk About You

What's keeping you from coming home right now?

*Aren't you tired of holding on to your anger?*

*Aren't you tired of trying so hard?*

*Aren't you tired of fighting?*

God isn't asking for your perfect performance. He's not even asking you to prove your love for Him. He's simply inviting you into His presence where you'll find the rest you're looking for. It's your heart He's interested in, not your talents or your treasure.

Will you risk quieting the noise in your head enough to hear Him say words you've longed to hear: "I have loved you with an everlasting love; therefore I have continued my faithfulness to you" (Jer. 31:3).

Anyone can start well. Everyone will face a messy middle. But it's how you *end* that matters the most.

Your story is far from over. God specializes in turnarounds. He did it for John Mark. He did it for the prodigal. He did it for me. And He's waiting to do it for you.

You've read this book for a reason. I don't believe in accidents. I don't believe in serendipitous luck. And I certainly don't believe that I'm a famous-enough author for you to have bought this book because of me.

The glorious truth you can't escape is that God is reconstructing your faith. God hasn't failed you. He's been right there all along, waiting for you to come home and He's holding up a sign that says:

Welcome back to Me!

**SPEND A FEW MINUTES CONSIDERING THESE QUESTIONS, and bring your thoughts and feelings to God in prayer:**

*When have you felt dissatisfied with Christianity?*

*Are you ready to say yes to God again?*

*Communicate honestly with God about your doubts, disappointments, and times when you have felt alone.*

# AFTERWORD

I had an epiphany the other day.

For years I've felt sorry for myself for not having my own big, romantic love story. For years I've wondered why God hadn't answered my prayers, until it occurred to me that *this* is my love story.

*This* is my big romance.

*This* is my very deep and very personal and very tender and now very public love story with Jesus.

If you have your own love story with Jesus, then you know exactly what I'm talking about.

And if you haven't started your own love story with Jesus, let this be your invitation to love.

Life is a great romance. It's the story of God wooing each of us toward Him. He longs for a love relationship with us, despite our brokenness. He pursues us even when we give Him every reason to stop.

His love never ends.

His love never changes.

His love is the only power strong enough to bend the most ardently resistant, and deep enough to penetrate the hardest hearts. And His love is whole enough to heal the most wounded among us. His love is what takes that which is deconstructed in your life and builds it up again.

His love is what made me whole again.

I warned you in the preface that this story wasn't going to be funny, but I hope it's been life-changing.

I hope that my story of Jesus' overwhelming, never-ending, reckless love for me has reignited your love for Him too.

Cheering you on,

Lina

# APPENDIX

# DECONSTRUCTION DIAGRAM

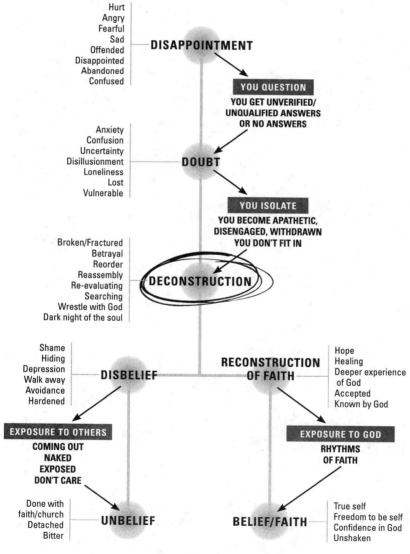

Hurt
Angry
Fearful
Sad
Offended
Disappointed
Abandoned
Confused

**DISAPPOINTMENT**

**YOU QUESTION**
**YOU GET UNVERIFIED/
UNQUALIFIED ANSWERS
OR NO ANSWERS**

Anxiety
Confusion
Uncertainty
Disillusionment
Loneliness
Lost
Vulnerable

**DOUBT**

**YOU ISOLATE**
**YOU BECOME APATHETIC,
DISENGAGED, WITHDRAWN
YOU DON'T FIT IN**

Broken/Fractured
Betrayal
Reorder
Reassembly
Re-evaluating
Searching
Wrestle with God
Dark night of the soul

**DECONSTRUCTION**

Shame
Hiding
Depression
Walk away
Avoidance
Hardened

**DISBELIEF**

**RECONSTRUCTION
OF FAITH**

Hope
Healing
Deeper experience
of God
Accepted
Known by God

**EXPOSURE TO OTHERS**
**COMING OUT
NAKED
EXPOSED
DON'T CARE**

**EXPOSURE TO GOD**
**RHYTHMS
OF FAITH**

Done with
faith/church
Detached
Bitter

**UNBELIEF**

**BELIEF/FAITH**

True self
Freedom to be self
Confidence in God
Unshaken

# ACKNOWLEDGMENTS

This book wouldn't have become a reality without Judy Dunagan from Moody Publishers, who asked me to dinner one day, then kept insisting I submit the proposal. I am grateful to the entire Moody team for yet another partnership with this book. Their trust is a gift I hold dearly.

I am particularly grateful to Amanda Cleary Eastep, my developmental editor, who at times proved she could even read my brain. I also want to thank Janis Backing, Ashley Torres, and Melissa Zaldivar from the marketing team at Moody.

Thank you to Jennifer Grant for her help in shaping and editing the early stages of this book.

I am grateful to my local church and my pastor Karl Clauson and his wife Junanne. They were instrumental in loving me at a time that I desperately needed it. I have always been and will continue to be a church girl despite a small detour that I've documented in the pages of this book. I'm also deeply grateful to Margo and Anita who continue to listen to me and point me back to God's love for me.

I am grateful to my family. They give me the freedom to live out my calling and have supported me through every season of my life.

One of these days I will meet the entire Living with Power community in person. Until then, I want to simply say thank you for the impact you have had on my life and calling. Your support of the work

God is doing in this ministry is so deep and faithful. A big thank you to the early readers group. You helped write this book. Thank you to my launch team! And thank you for my ministry leadership team including Joy and Janice!

I have the privilege of calling Don Pape my literary agent and friend. What a gift he has been to me. He has taken this project to the next level. I look forward to many more projects with him in the future.

I am grateful to Tina Watschke for being the best friend a girl could ask for. I would like to publicly acknowledge her for coming up with the title for this book. It's a long story, but she basically saved the day.

Last but not least, let it be known that were it not for my sister Diana and my assistant Irina, I might be living in Tahiti right now— all by my lonesome self. They have talked me off the ledge more times than I can count. They have loved me unconditionally. They have continued to pour themselves out for the sake of the Lord tirelessly and joyfully. It is a privilege and honor to do life with them.

Finally, to Jesus. This book has been all about You and for You. Thank You for loving me.

# NOTES

## Chapter 1: Where Is God in My Pain?

1. C. S. Lewis, *The Problem of Pain* (San Francisco: HarperOne, 2001), 91.

2. St. John of the Cross, *The Ascent of Mount Carmel*, trans. David Lewis (London: Baker, 1906) and *The Dark Night of the Soul*, trans. Gabriela Cunninghame Graham (London: Watkins, 1905).

## Chapter 2: Why Did My Story End Up This Way?

1. "Americans Divided on the Importance of Church," Barna Group, March 24, 2014, https://www.barna.com/research/americans-divided-on-the-importance-of-church/; Christine Emba, "Opinion: Why Millennials Are Skipping Church and Not Going Back," *Washington Post*, October 27, 2019, https://www.washingtonpost.com/opinions/why-millennials-are-skipping-church-and-not-going-back/2019/10/27/0d35b972-f777-11e9-8cf0-4cc99f74d127_story.html.

2. Pew Research Center, "In U.S., Decline of Christianity Continues at Rapid Pace," Pew Research Center, October 17, 2019, https://www.pewforum.org/2019/10/17/in-u-s-decline-of-christianity-continues-at-rapid-pace.

## Chapter 3: Why Can't I Overcome Sin in My Life?

1. This saying appears to be based on lyrics from the song "Sin Will Take You Farther" by Christian and gospel singer Harold McWhorter. https://www.shazam.com/track/64356548/sin-will-take-you-farther.

2. Timothy Keller with Kathy Keller, *The Meaning of Marriage: Facing the Complexities of Commitment with the Wisdom of God* (New York: Penguin Books, 2011), 44.

3. John Piper, "Why Do I Keep Sinning?," Desiring God, October 15, 2018, https://www.desiringgod.org.

## Chapter 5: Is God Really Fair?

1. "Americans Divided on the Importance of Church," Barna Group, March 24, 2014, https://www.barna.com/research/americans-divided-on-the-importance-of-church/; Christine Emba, "Opinion: Why Millennials Are Skipping Church and Not Going Back," *Washington Post*, October 27, 2019, https://www.washingtonpost.com /opinions/why-millennials-are-skipping-church-and-not-going-back/2019/10/27/0d35b972-f777-11e9-8cf0-4cc99f74d127_story.html.

2. Elyse Pham, "How Christian Singer's Life Has Changed since Revealing He No Longer Believes in God," *Today*, October 6, 2020, https://www.today.com/popculture/how-jon-steingard-s-life-has-changed-revealing-he-no-t192211.

3. "John Steingard," Instagram, https://www.instagram.com/p/CAbHm10lt7w.

4. Ibid.

5. C. S. Lewis, *God in the Dock* (Grand Rapids, MI: Wm. B. Eerdmans Publishing Co., 2014), 268.

## Chapter 6: Is *This* the Normal Christian Life?

1. "El-Elohe-Israel," BibleGateway, https://www.biblegateway.com/resources/encyclopedia-of-the-bible/El-Elohe-Israel.

## Chapter 7: Why Can't I Feel More of God in My Life?

1. Dallas Willard, as quoted in John Ortberg, *Soul Keeping: Caring for the Most Important Part of You* (Grand Rapids, MI: Zondervan, 2014), 20.

## Chapter 8: Why Is It Hard for Christians to Love?

1. Warren W. Wiersbe, *On Being a Leader for God* (Grand Rapids, MI: Baker Books, 2011), 39.

2. Original source not found.

Tired of feeling sorry for yourself?
Sick of answering the same old questions about
why you still haven't found your perfect match?

# HAVE YOU EVER SERIOUSLY QUESTIONED CHRISTIANITY?

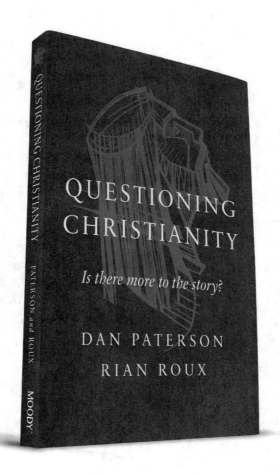

# DOUBTING GOD IS NORMAL.
# BUT CONFIDENCE IN HIM IS POSSIBLE.

**MOODY Publishers®**

*From the Word to Life®*

*Without a Doubt* is for anyone who wrestles with whether their faith is well-grounded or the promises of Christianity are true. Pastor Dean Inserra lays out what the Bible teaches about how to have saving faith in God. You'll learn the clear truth about what a Christian is—and what a Christian is not.

978-0-8024-2360-3    |    also available as eBook and audiobook

# ENCOUNTER GOD
# AND WORSHIP HIM MORE DEEPLY.

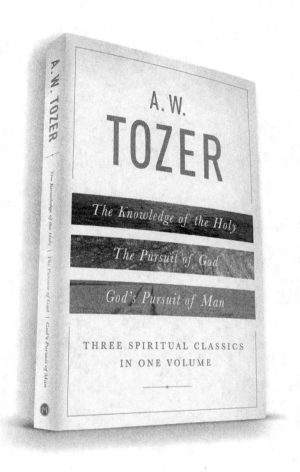